Police
Operations

Police Operations

Mukesh Singh (IPS)
Viplav Kumar Choudhry (IPS)

Manas Publications
(We Convert Fighters into Writers)
New Delhi - 110 002 (INDIA)

MANAS PUBLICATIONS
(We Convert Fighters into Writers)
(Publishers - Library Suppliers - Importers & Exporters)
4402/5-A, Ansari Road (Opp. HDFC Bank)
Darya Ganj, New Delhi - 110 002 (India)
Off.: 011-40198110, Fax: 011-23272766
E-mail : manaspublications@gmail.com

2nd Impression 2026 (FP - 2015)

ISBN : 978-81-7049-509-3

₹ 795/-

Designed by
Manas Publications

Printed in India at
R.K. Print Services, Delhi

Published by Mrs Suman Lata for
Manas Publications
4402/5-A, Ansari Road (Opp HDFC Bank),
Darya Ganj, New Delhi - 110 002 (INDIA)

To

the memories

of

Our Colleagues

in

the Jammu and Kashmir Police

who

attained martyrdom

while

fighting the terrorists

along with us.

Foreword

In the days to come the greatest challenge to India's development is going to be the increased security threat. As the concept of conventional war is going to die down slowly, countries inimical to Indian interests will resort to asymmetric warfare. The challenge in asymmetric war is that our own people are pitted against us. What a better way of doing it, than to exploit sentiment based on selective interpretations of religion and history to create a sense of grievance and then use it to create terrorist situations. This has entirely led to a paradigm shift in the task that is before the police and has added yet another dimension to its multiple tasks.

The operations that have been reviewed in this book would be useful to the officers of police and para-military forces in dealing with any security situation, without inflicting any collateral damage. Failure to respect human rights leads to a greater perception of oppression and only adds to the supporters of insurgency.

With a large number of States affected by extremist violence, the country's police force will need to rise to the challenge and therefore would need to be better equipped, both in terms of training and weaponry to deal with the emerging situation.

I hope this book will help police officers to understand the kind of situations that can develop while fighting terrorists and how they have to be dealt with taking utmost care not to afflict collateral damage, both in terms of human life and property. In many instances there has to be a compromise to ensure that the terrorists are not allowed to get away but in the balance of convenience, under no circumstances, should there be a compromise on human life. In all cases opportunity must be given to the terrorist to surrender, who is holed up.

The J&K Police has been on the forefront in fighting terrorists from the very beginning. After the initial onslaught of the militants it took the police a few years to re-group themselves. But after the formation of the Special Operations Group, the police took on the leadership role and in the process has contributed significantly to minimize terrorist activities in Kashmir. This has not come on a small price but with sacrifices of 920 officers and men, made by the police would be amongst the highest of any police force in the country. The officers have sacrificed their personal lives and comfort for the national cause. The refinement in the operations and minimizing human rights violations was possible only when the J&K Police took on the leadership role.

Authors of this book—Shri Mukesh Singh and Shri Viplav Kumar Choudhry—worked under me as Superintendents of Police in sensitive districts of Kashmir. Both of them are highly sophisticated police officers, who fully comprehend the multi-dimensional role that needs to be played by an Indian police officer in the current security environment. They themselves led operations and even had narrow escapes during encounters. Their bravery is an example for the police force and an inspiration to the younger officers. I have closely observed both of them in meticulously planning operations to the last detail and leading them personally.

Both the officers have worked in the National Human Rights Commission and are familiar with the requirements of India's objectives in maintaining respect to the human rights.

It is necessary that in keeping with democratic principles, the importance of human rights is not forgotten. In the days to come, one of the weapons that will be used against the police force will be accusations of human rights violations against police officers. Pseudo human rights organizations will be coming to the fore with the objective to defame the police organization. It is, therefore, necessary that precautions, as advised in this book, are fully taken so as to ensure that our men and officers do not become victim of such attempts.

SM Sahai
(IG, Kashmir Police)

Preface

A large portion of the country today is facing threats from the terrorists, insurgents, Naxalites and such other anti-national elements, often challenging the legitimate authority of the State. In some parts of the country, these elements have been even putting up serious threats to the integrity of the nation.

Police personnel working in such areas often come face-to-face with such elements who are armed with sophisticated weapons and are well-trained in handling such arms and ammunition. Even in other parts of the country which are not affected by the menace of terrorism or insurgency, police personnel often have to deal with the armed offenders.

In such face-off with the armed offenders, the police have to often resort to use force and the police personnel find themselves in situations involving exchange of firing with the armed offenders. Law permits use of lethal force by the police, but the rights of the police to use force is not unlimited. It is rather restricted and subject to some limitations, and use of force by the police, if not justified in accordance with the provisions of law, may result in the police personnel being held for having committed a criminal offence or human rights violation.

The objective of this book is basically to impress upon the police personnel to follow the legal provisions related to use of force while conducting a police operation. To give a good perspective about the police operations, planning and execution of a police operation which may result in use of force by the police while dealing with armed offenders, has been discussed in detail. Besides, the legal position related to the use of force while dealing with armed offenders, with which the police officers should be well-acquainted, have also been discussed to give a complete perspective to the reader. Emphasis has been more on to make a police officer understand the importance of conducting proper investigation of an incident involving use of force by the police, from legal as well as from human rights point of view. These important points have been illustrated through case studies. Acts and provisions of law—national as well as international—in abridged form, have been added in the appendix to make the reader aware of legal provisions relevant to use of force in police operations.

This book is primarily meant for the officers of the level of District Superintendent of Police, Deputy Superintendent of Police and police officers of the rank of Inspectors/Sub-Inspectors who are often required to lead the police party in a police operation. Officers at the similar levels in the para-military police forces and other Armed forces would also find this book useful. This book would be particularly beneficial for the officers entering into the police service at the leadership levels—Indian Police Service officers, Deputy Superintendent of Police in various State police services, and those joining the police service at Sub-Inspector level. We hope, it would give them a good insight into planning and execution of police operations, particularly in the beginning, besides understanding the legal dimensions associated with the police operations. Those not belonging to the police or a security force may also find this book interesting, to get a good perspective on the police operations.

We are immensely grateful to our colleagues in the Jammu & Kashmir Police, working with whom for long years gave us a good experience in planning and executing police operations. Sincere thanks are also due to our colleagues in the National Investigation Agency (NIA) and the National Human Rights Commission (NHRC) working with whom has been an enriching experience.

We express our heartfelt gratitude to Prof BT Kaul of Faculty of Law, Delhi University for giving us valuable suggestions regarding the legal perspectives on use of force in police operations. We gratefully acknowledge his contributions on the legal analysis of the issues—'homicide' and 'right of private defence'—which have been mentioned in this book.

We categorically state that the narration/views etc. mentioned in this book are purely of ours and are based on our perception of the situation and resemblance, if any, with actual incidents, is purely coincidental.

Mukesh Singh
Viplav Kumar Choudhry

Contents

Annexures

CHAPTER 1

Planning and Conducting an Operation

There are different situations during a police operation in which the police is compelled to use lethal force, be it a planned counter insurgency/counter terrorism operation or a chance face off with an armed terrorist. In each of these situations there are a set of basic rules which have to be followed and another set of variables which have to be controlled, depending upon peculiarity of the police operation.

In an intelligence based operation, time is the most crucial factor while planning the operation. The time available with the police for planning and execution of an operation usually varies from one hour to twenty four hours. In rare circumstances the time period available for planning and execution can be more. Limited time available to the police leadership therefore, throws many challenges. Variables like terrain of the area, type of population, time of the day when the information came in, whether in an inhabited area or in an open area, reliability of the source, strength of the terrorists/insurgents/criminals, strength of manpower available for the operation and availability of resources such as weaponry and vehicles have to be considered before any operation is launched.

In other cases, for example in case of an ambush situation also police may be required to use lethal force but in this case the only parameter which is in the control of the police party (if they have been ambushed) would be prior preparedness of the police party and their knowledge of the terrain. Other aspects of the response of the police party in an ambush situation would depend upon the variables such as site of the ambush, timing of the ambush, number of terrorists carrying out the ambush, type of weapons being used by the terrorists, and objective of the terrorists. On the other hand, in a police operation where an ambush has been laid by the police forces, almost all the parameters would be in control of the police party.

This chapter emphasizes importance of taking care of the basic rules and the need of controlling the variables in different situations in which the police may be forced to use lethal force. This has been done with the help of case studies which are based on actual incidents. Cases of a well-planned intelligence based cordon and search operation, case of a 'Fidayeen attack' (suicide attack), case of an ambush, case of use of force in an operation in an urban area, case of use of force in an operation in a rural area, case of use of force in an operation involving a religious place, case of a hostage situation and case of a law and order problem during use of force in an operation have been analysed in this chapter.

To make a simpler understanding of the parameters to be taken care of in a police operation involving use of force, the entire situation has been divided into three parts: before launch of the operation, during the operation, and after the operation. While planning and during the subsequent execution of a police operation, these aspects need to be specially taken care of by the police leadership.

Planning an Operation

The first thing which needs to be considered before deciding to launch an operation is to make a proper assessment of the intelligence available. Is it specific regarding a particular house or regarding presence of terrorists in a general area such as a village? Is it regarding a group of terrorists or regarding an individual terrorist? These are important parameters for deciding strategy for launching an operation.

Reliability of the source providing the operation is of prime importance. If he has provided good information in the past then his reliability would definitely be high. On many occasions however, the source is an individual who has come to provide information about the terrorists for the first time. Truthfulness of such source can be assessed by his motive for giving information about the terrorists. Money is usually a prime consideration for majority of the sources. Reliability of a source, who has come to provide information due to some personal grudge against a particular terrorist, would however, normally be higher. Further, if a source is willing to accompany the police party during the operation then such source would definitely be more reliable. It is also possible to ascertain the reliability of a source from his expressions while narrating the information. For instance, if he is looking scared or is shivering, likelihood of the information provided by him being true would be higher.

Proper assessment of reliability of the source is important as a source can even be a trap planted by the terrorists and can cause damages to the police party if an operation is planned based on his tainted 'intelligence'. Terrorists can also take advantage of the situation if they get knowledge about a particular source working for the police. For instance, on one occasion, a very reliable source who was tested may times before, gave information about presence of terrorists in a village where three terrorists, according to his inputs, were supposed to be hiding during the night time. Based on the information, the Superintendent of Police (Operations) sent a police party along with a column of the CRPF to the village at night. The informer insisted that the police party must stop at a place where they would see a bicycle with a bag and then wait for the source who would then give the exact information. Police party reached close to the village and upon spotting a bicycle parked near a culvert when they stopped and waited for the source, a powerful IED (Improvised Explosive Device) exploded below the culvert leading to casualties of one officer and five other security force personnel. The DySP (Operations) leading the police party barely managed to survive. It was later found that the terrorists had come to know about the police source and had taken him into captivity. He was made to make calls to the SP (Operations) from captivity regarding the presence of the terrorists. The calls were made out of fear and finally led to huge casualties on the police side. The source was also killed later by the terrorists. Although the source was time tested and had given reliable information in the past, the fact that he was providing information at odd hours, coupled with the fact that he did not disclose the entire information at one time, should have raised suspicion about the source and a careful analysis of the information could have saved precious lives.

Likewise, a new source who has never provided any information to the police needs to be always viewed with suspicion. In such a situation the information is either likely to be hundred percent true or it is equally likely to be a trap. The following incident would substantiate this point. Here a lady known to an Assistant Sub-Inspector (ASI) of the 'Special Operation Group' of the police was won over by the terrorists. On one occasion she provided information to the ASI about presence of one terrorist commander near her house. According to the information, the terrorist was in the neighbouring house and was only having a pistol. Since the target was important and according to the information very lightly armed, in the excitement, the ASI along with a Sub-

Inspector (SI) decided to conduct the operation with a small police party and went out with only three of their colleagues in a civil vehicle. Before leaving, they intimated the colour of the vehicle and make of the vehicle to the lady informant. When the vehicle was negotiating a steep bend close to the village, the police party was ambushed by heavily armed terrorists in which the young SI laid down his life. Two other policemen also got injured in the incident.

As mentioned earlier, one important aspect to be considered while analysing the importance of a source is the motivation of the source in giving the information. A regular time tested source who provides information for monetary considerations takes a chance and may also provide general information based on hearsay which can be wrong. On the other hand, if the source has come to the police due to personal reasons, likelihood of the information being true is very high. Take for instance the following case. A source from a very remote village came to the Superintendent of Police (SP) of the district with information regarding presence of ten terrorists in his village. He was a first time source who was earlier reported to be very close to the terrorists. It was also reported that he had made many underground hideouts for the terrorists. The SP viewed the source with suspicion and thought that this might be a trap laid by the terrorists since it was the maize crop season and chances of ambush during the process of reaching to the village was very high. When the source was asked about his motive behind coming to the police, he disclosed that one of the terrorist commanders wanted to marry his sister by force to which she was not ready. He said that he had made the hideouts himself and wanted all the terrorists to be killed. He also informed that the terrorists would not run away seeing the police party since no one knew about the hideouts. He said that on many previous occasions, the police parties had crossed the area without noticing presence of the terrorists. The information appeared credible and the SP asked the source to accompany the police party at night while laying the cordon. The source willingly got dressed up like a police personnel and accompanied the police party. He led the police to five hideouts of the terrorists and in the operation all the ten terrorists got killed while one policeman also sacrificed his life.

Protection of the 'source' who agrees to accompany the police party is very important because if his identity is disclosed—chances of which is more in case he accompanies the police party during the operation and gets opportunity to interact with the police personnel in the operation party—he would become a target of the terrorists. In the operation also, since he leads the police party to a place being used by the terrorists as their hideout, there is a great risk to the life of the source as he may come in the cross firing between the terrorists and the police party.

An important point is that while going for even a small operation in a militancy affected area, all the 'routine' precautions must be taken, else an operation planned in haste or without observing the basic rules can lead to serious damages to the operation party. For instance, any movement of the police party in a sensitive area should be in at least two vehicles which should maintain some distance between them during the movement and should move in such a manner that police personnel in a vehicle can see the police party in the other vehicles. This helps in case the party is ambushed by the terrorists while moving. In such circumstances in case of firing by the terrorists on one of the moving vehicles, police personnel in the other vehicle get opportunity to effectively retaliate the attack and give covering protection to the vehicle being fired upon.

While going for the operation the police officer leading the operation should plan for the alternative strategies also in advance, in case some problems are encountered in the one being acted upon during the operation. The leader of the operation should properly plan and launch the operation with manpower and weaponry besides other resources, sufficient to take on the terrorists/insurgents/criminals. Situation can be different in a covert operation where the terrorist is taken by surprise and does not get the time to react. However, in a cordon and search type of operation police party should be of sufficient strength and equipped with adequate weaponry and other resources such as bullet-proof jackets and night vision devices (in case the operation is launched during the night hours or in cases where the cordon is expected to be continued during the night time). In one incident, in-charge of the police post located in a remote rural area received information about presence of a freshly infiltrated group of five terrorists in a village. The police post was poorly manned with strength of only twenty police personnel and they were not very well equipped. The Sub-Inspector in-charge of the police post however decided to take on the terrorists in the difficult hilly terrain with this limited strength and fire-power. He immediately sent a wireless message for reinforcement from the district headquarters and in the meanwhile left for the spot where the terrorists were reportedly hiding. The police party reached the spot after about an hour of arduous trek but before they could properly lay the cordon, the terrorists spotted them and fired heavily resulting in injuries to two policemen. The SI however re-grouped his men and ensured that the terrorists did not get chance to escape. The policeman holding the only Light Machine Gun (LMG) available with the police party efficiently operated the LMG before laying down his life while trying to remove a temporary block in his machine gun. Four terrorists got killed in the exchange of firing. By the time reinforcements reached the site, it was too late as the operation had ended and one policeman had laid down his life and four others were injured. The policemen indeed acted very bravely during the operation but the precious lives of three policemen could have been possibly saved had the operation been conducted with a bigger police party with adequate fire-power, matching those of the terrorists.

Before launching the operation the police party must be properly briefed. Important aspects of an operation like how and where the vehicles carrying the police party should stop, which police party should lay the outer cordon and which police party should conduct house search or should lay the inner cordon should be decided in advance and the police personnel taking part in the operation should be briefed accordingly. Maps can be of great help in briefing the police party for an operation in the urban area while sand models can be of help in case of an operation in a mountainous area. Further, communication between the police party by the use of wireless sets or mobile phones during the operation should be properly planned and checked in advance. Carrying of a public address system such as a loud hailer proves to be useful in addressing the locals who usually gather around the site of the operation, particularly in urban areas. Such a system also comes very handy sometimes, for giving information to the media personnel present on the site.

Conducting an Operation

Upon reaching the place where the terrorists are suspected to be hiding, vehicles should be stopped a little away from the suspected place and moving on foot, the police party first of all should establish an outer cordon quickly so that the terrorists do not get any opportunity to escape in the first go itself upon noticing presence of a police party. Police personnel should invariably be deployed in 'buddy pairs' so that each could give protection to his 'buddy' in case of an attack by the hiding terrorists. 'Buddy pair' system of deployment also helps in maintaining more alertness in police personnel who are deployed in the cordon.

In case the cordon continues even during the night, as it is safer to suspend the operation after the sunset and resume it after the sunrise the next day, the cordon around the suspected area should be properly laid. Police men deployed for the cordon should be rotated in case they have been performing duties for long hours. The area should also be secured by putting barbed/concertina wire. Further, the area should also be kept well lit by making temporary lighting arrangements. The time between 2-4 AM is the most crucial period as the holed up terrorists try to escape during this period taking advantage of darkness and tiredness of the policemen.

House search is the most crucial part of any operation. Maximum casualties can be caused by the terrorists hiding in the house when the search party enters inside the house. This is primarily because the terrorists may be aware of the location and movements of the policemen entering in the house but the policemen in the search party are not aware of the place where the terrorist might be hiding. House search should therefore be done by the policemen who are highly trained for this purpose. In one of the operations conducted in a village, during the operation, when the police party was trying to enter in the suspected house, one of the policemen was dragged inside the house by the terrorists and was kept hostage. Thereafter, the operation had to be stopped because any action on the part of the police could have potentially harmed the policeman taken inside the house by the terrorists. One more policeman sustained injuries in the attempt to rescue the trapped policeman. Subsequently after great efforts, when the terrorists hiding inside the house got killed, the police party somehow managed to enter inside the house but by then the trapped policeman had been killed by the terrorists and his dead body only could be retrieved from the house. Similarly, in another operation launched by the police in a village when the police party was searching a house, a suspected hideout was noticed. When a constable of the search party tried to uncover the hideout, the terrorists hiding inside the hideout pulled him inside from his head. Other policemen tried to protect him and in the process half of his body got inside the hideout while the rest half, from the side of the leg, remained outside, the police men trying to pull him out. Needless to say that the police constable could not be saved.

Further, extreme care should be taken in case of an operation involving a religious place as in such a situation, any damage to the religious place may flare up religious sentiments which can lead to major law and order problems not only in that particular place but also across the entire area. Such operations should therefore be handled in a very tactful manner. Locals and the religious heads of the area should also be taken into confidence during such operations. Further, during the search operation, steps should be taken in order to prevent entry of terrorists in the religious laces. For instance, in a case on information about presence of terrorists, an operation was launched by the police in a village. During search of the houses in the village, the terrorists present in the village, upon noticing presence of the police party and finding no scope to escape, entered in the village mosque. The police party soon noticed the terrorists having taken shelter inside the mosque but their action got limited as it would have resulted into damages to the mosque. Due to these considerations the police party later withdrew from the village, calling off the operation despite having suffered two casualties. The situation could have been avoided and the terrorists could have been prevented from entering in the mosque, had a small police party been deployed close to the mosque at the time of establishing of the cordon itself.

The strategy which should be adopted in a particular operation depends to a large extent on the place where the operation is to be carried out. In comparison to a rural area one needs to take more precautions in an urban area. The terrorists generally prefer to stay in a place where they have a support base in the local population. In such areas, during the operation, sympathizers of the terrorists may try to create law and order problems in order to distract the police engaged in the operation. A police party while operating in a thickly populated urban area should therefore, necessarily have a law and order component to deal with such eventualities. Secondly, the chance of damages to civilians or to their property in case of an operation in a populated area is much more. Damages to the civilians during the operation such as damage to the houses of civilians or civilian casualties in the cross-firing during the operation should be avoided as it not only results in adverse publicity against the police party for human rights violations, it may also result in law and order problems subsequently.

The police officer leading the operation should therefore be very careful and take utmost care to avoid casualties of the civilians and damages to their properties. Policemen should be properly briefed in advance and also prior arrangement should be done for making available fire brigades on the spot in order to deal with a possible situation of fire which may occur during the operation.

Further, during the operation the leader of the police party should focus more on directing and coordinating with his men.

Control on firing by the policemen should be given due importance as in case of an uncontrolled firing in a situation involving exchange of firing between the police and the armed offenders the chances of damages to the civilians can be more. Besides, there can be casualties to the operation party itself. Situation can be more complicated in case policemen from different units are involved in an operation who may not know each other. In such a situation a system should be devised before start of the operation so as to communicate with leaders of each of the police party. Most important aspect to be taken care of by the police officer leading the operation is to keep all the police men under his command alert and properly control them. Bravery is desired but not foolhardiness. A terrorist can be taken on later also, but losing men in an operation can greatly affect morale of the police party for a long time.

During a search operation, whether in a particular house or during a general search in all the suspected houses in a locality, after the house search is over, sympathizers of the terrorists may level false charges against the police party for having taken some valuables from the house or for having misbehaved with the ladies. In order to avoid such false accusations, local representatives or the village Headman should invariably be associated during the search operation by the police party, while ensuring his safety. Further, civilians should be treated with due courtesy while conducting searches. Women should be searched only by lady police personnel, or in absence of lady police, by a local lady. If possible, the local Magistrate should also be associated during the search operation after the cordon has been laid down. In case of non-availability of a Magistrate during the operation efforts should be made for presence of the Magistrate at the site of the operation as soon as possible.

However, under no circumstances civilians should be used as a shield against the terrorists during the operation or while conducting search.

After the Operation

After the operation ends there is a general tendency that the police personnel become relaxed and even a little casual. However, even at this stage of the operation there can be possibilities of damages being caused to the police party. The first aspect needs to be taken care of after an operation ends is the handling of the dead body of the killed terrorist. Important point here is how to approach the 'dead body' of the presumably dead terrorist as the 'dead' terrorist may in fact be alive, pretending to be dead, waiting for the last opportunity to cause damages to the police party and may inflict casualties to the policemen approaching the 'dead body'. In case the 'dead' terrorist is lying on the ground on his chest, it is always safer to approach him from his leg side as in this scenario, if he is approached from the head side, if alive, he can see the police personnel approaching him and can cause damages to them. But if he is approached from his leg side, he cannot see the police personnel approaching him. On the same logic, if the 'dead' terrorist is lying on his back with his face up, it is safer to approach him from his head side.

Careful handling of dead body of a killed terrorist is also important as a terrorist may be having an unexploded grenade in his hand which he could not have thrown at the last minute after removing its pin and the grenade remained in his fist, with its lever pressed, due to development of cadaveric spasm. It may also happen that during the operation the terrorist might have taken out the pin of the grenade but could not throw it and the grenade remained unexploded as the lever of the grenade remain pressed due to body weight of the killed terrorist. In this case the grenade may explode when during the process of removal of the dead body lever of the grenade becomes free once the bodyweight is removed. In one of the incidents, after conclusion of the operation, the police party had gathered together to get a photograph clicked in front of the dead body of a killed terrorist. As the body was turned, a grenade under the body exploded causing serious injuries to thirty seven police personnel, thus turning the celebrations into mourning. One policeman later succumbed to his injuries. Similarly, in another case, a dead body of a terrorist lying in a village was reported during the night hours and the next day a police team from the Police Station brought dead body of the killed terrorist to the police station. Dead body of the terrorist was kept in the premises of the police station and senior police officers including the District Superintendent of Police (SP) came to the police station to see the dead body. There was a pouch on the body of the dead terrorist (generally kept by the terrorists for carrying arms and ammunition). A police constable removed the pouch from the dead body by cutting it with a blade and thereafter while he was trying to open the button of the pouch, a grenade kept in the pouch exploded causing serious injuries to the police personnel present around the dead body including the district SP.

The spot where the operation has taken place, and its surrounding areas, should be properly cleared before withdrawal of the police party from the place after the operation is over. This is necessary as there may be unexploded explosive materials such as hand grenades used during the operation either by the police party or by the terrorist. Such explosives, if not detected and if remain at the spot after the operation, may cause damage to the civilians visiting the area later. Site of the operation therefore should be properly sanitized through the bomb disposal units, before the police party withdraws from the site of operation.

After any operation, withdrawal from the spot should be tactical. The route should be properly sanitized. If a proper ROP (Road Opening Party) cannot be deployed on the route to be taken while returning, the route can be made safe to some extent by conducting vehicle patrolling on the route using bullet proof vehicles. Preferably, the whole operation party should not move out together; instead they should move in small groups. Also, while returning the police party should necessarily choose a route other than the one used for going to the spot. In case there is only one approach to the spot, the timing of withdrawal after the operation should have a surprise element. This is necessary since after the police party goes to the spot for carrying out an operation, the terrorists come to know about their presence in that particular area and may be on a look out to get opportunity for attacking the police party during the time of withdrawal. Thus, the chances of an ambush while withdrawing from the operation site are more. In such circumstances, prior preparedness of the police party and strict adherence to the vehicular movement drill greatly enhances effectiveness of the response of the police party. On many occasions terrorists have inflicted casualties on the police party during withdrawal. In one of the incidents in a village two civilians were killed by the terrorists during night time. One of the two civilians, a government employee, was killed by the terrorists on the allegation of being a 'source' of the police, while the other was killed because of being the 'Panch' (elected representative from the village in the 'Panchayat', a local body). Since the village was located in a highly militancy affected area, next day a strong police party of strength 23 including a photographer and two medical assistants were deputed from the Police Station to the village under the command of a Sub-Inspector of police for conducting investigations and other formalities. All the police personnel and the civilian staff were in a single TATA-407 vehicle. After conducting preliminary investigations and completing procedural formalities when the police party was coming back to the police station, at about 4 PM, heavily armed terrorists ambushed the police vehicle. In the attack 14 police personnel and the two civilian staff of the Medical Department got killed while rest of the 9 police personnel sustained serious injuries. The terrorists also looted arms and ammunition of the police personnel and decamped with the wireless set fitted in the police vehicle after setting the police vehicle on fire. It was obvious in this case that the terrorists had information that the police party would return to the police station after conducting their investigation/formalities taking the only possible route to the police station. Damage to the police party would definitely have been less had the police party been travelling in two or three vehicles, with some distance between the vehicles, as the police personnel in the vehicle, not in the range of firing by the terrorists could have effectively retaliated the firing by the terrorists.

Another aspect of the police operation, after the operation is over, is debriefing of the police personnel who took part in the operation. Very often this aspect is ignored due to the fatigue factor. All the police personnel are eager to get back to home and take rest after a long drawn operation. Debriefing session, to be conducted by the leader of the police party, is necessary as it gives the police personnel an opportunity to do introspection about their strength and shortcomings, and the way they conducted the operation. This exercise, conducted immediately after the operation, leaves a lasting impression in the minds of the force which helps them avoid repeating the mistakes if any, committed during the operation.

These points have been elaborated with the help of the case studies discussed in the succeeding portion of the book.

CASE STUDIES

1. Operation in the Capital City

1. This incident happened just a day prior to the day of polling for the all-important assembly elections in the city affected by terrorism. That day, the nearby CRPF (Central Reserve Police Force) Commandant met the SP City and informed that he had some intelligence inputs regarding suicide attack at Polytechnic Institute Camp where distribution of electronic voting machines was to take place. About three hundred polling officers had assembled in the Polytechnic camp, which was guarded by a CISF (Central Industrial Security Force) platoon, deployed for the election duty. This CISF platoon which was accommodated in tents in the ground of the Polytechnic Institute, had recently come from Delhi and did not have any previous experience of working in the terrorism affected areas. They were also not adequately sufficiently equipped in terms of weaponry to handle a terrorist attack.
2. The information provided by the Commandant of the nearby CRPF unit was regarding presence of two terrorists of suicide squad of a terrorist outfit in the houses adjoining Polytechnic Institute. This CRPF unit was not in charge of the polytechnic camp but was meant to guard the nearby stadium and residence of VIPs adjoining the stadium where most of the important government functions were held. The SP City did not take the information very seriously because a large number of generic inputs were being received by the police in a routine manner regarding presence of the terrorists in the city just before the elections.

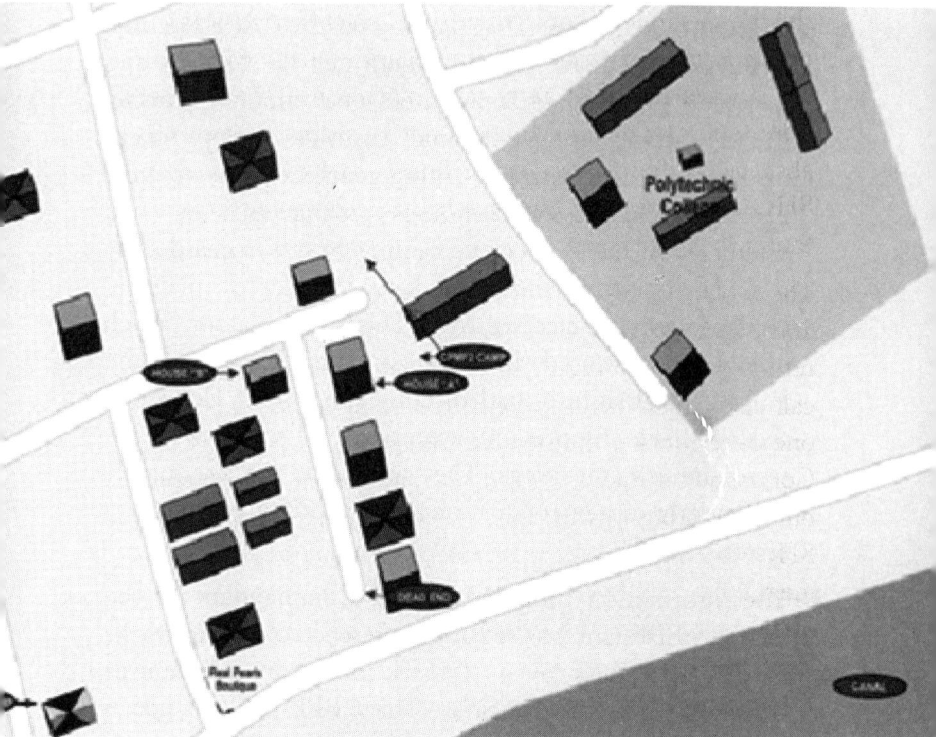

Operation in the Capital City.

3. The SP City, however, mustered strength of three platoons comprising of one platoon of CRPF and two platoons of BSF (Border Security Force) from the camps situated nearby along with his own men including the local Station House Officer (SHO) and the Sub-Divisional Police Officer (SDPO) and searched the general area adjoining the Polytechnic camp. Since the exact house was not pointed out, the police and the security forces searched all the houses in the vicinity with attention. Three houses were found locked which could not be searched due to the absence of the owners of the house. The SDPO and the SHO reported after the search that nothing adverse was found during the search.
4. The CRPF Commandant was then accordingly informed and after meeting with the Commandant, the SP City returned to his office. Within a span of fifteen minutes, a call again came from the CRPF Commandant saying that one of the locked houses was not searched properly. The Commandant, however, did not give any specific reason, but on hearing this SP City got suspicious and asked the SHO to call the owner of the concerned house. In the meantime, two more officers of CRPF also reached the office of SP City and offered their help. Considering the fact that there were other forces also present nearby, the SP City informed the local BSF Commandant in order to avoid confusion.
5. The area of that specific house and 2-3 more houses in the vicinity was cordoned off. The CISF Unit in the Polytechnic camp was also informed regarding the search. They were given the responsibility to cordon the area from the side of Polytechnic. The owner of the locked house was called to the site and asked to accompany the security forces to help open the lock of his house for conducting

search. He told the SP City that he was feeling scared due to the presence of the security forces and also that he had heart problem. When asked about the presence of any terrorist inside the house, he pleaded ignorance and said that he had locked the house himself in the morning and nobody was present inside. The SP City requested all the three officers of the CRPF and the officer of BSF for establishing a tight cordon and also to join for search along with his own staff. Teams were divided to cover the outer cordon and one officer of CRPF joined the SP City with his own PSOs to search the house. After taking permission from the owner of the house, the lock on the door of the house was broke open. SP City along with SDPO city and the SHO entered the house which was three-storied and started carrying out the search. Common places, particularly the 'Hamam' and the kitchen, where the terrorists usually hide in the urban areas were searched with special attention. Search of the ground floor and first floor of the house were completed during which nothing suspicious was found. It was perceived by this time that most probably the information received was false. The SP City, however, insisted that whole house be searched properly. There was a bathroom outside the house which was left untouched. The officer of CRPF and SP City himself went down to search the bathroom to check any possibility of presence of terrorists hiding there. Meanwhile, the police personnel searched the second floor in a very casual manner thinking that the information was not correct.

6. When the SP City and officer of the CRPF were busy in searching the bathroom area outside, sound of gunshots was heard from the second floor along with sound of explosion of grenades. The SP City ran towards the house where he found one of his own PSO (Personal Security

Officer) lying down with a bullet injury. Explosion of grenades and heavy firing was still going on and it was not possible to enter the house to assess the situation inside the house. Immediate task was to evacuate the injured Constable and give him first aid. The SP City signalled to the BSF bullet-proof bunker vehicle to come inside the premises of the house so that the injured Constable could be evacuated. However, the vehicle could not be moved inside the boundary of the house since the gate of the house was not big enough for a large vehicle. The SP City then asked the driver of his own bullet-proof Gypsy to come inside and the police personnel accompanying him managed to pull out the injured Constable.

7. By now it was clear that there were two terrorists hiding inside. It was also noticed that three policemen namely the SDPO, SHO and the Wireless Operator of the SP City were missing. The injured Constable had succumbed to his injuries on way to the hospital. Senior officers of police and other security forces came to the spot. A large number of media personnel who had come to the city to cover the assembly elections, also gathered near the spot.

8. There was a state of chaos at the spot. Despite being repeatedly asked to surrender, the terrorists did not accept the request of the policemen and instead kept firing intermittently from the house. In the meanwhile a large number of senior officers from the CRPF, BSF and the Police, three of the rank of Inspector Generals, four of the rank of Deputy Inspector Generals, five Commandants and others of lower ranks, had come to the spot and started briefing their respective forces, which added to the confusion even more. The operation party was losing precious time before the sunset to take on the terrorist. Gathering of a large number of senior officers in a house

close to the spot could have been a potential target for another suicide attack. It became dark after sometime. The lights of house where all the senior officers had gathered were purposefully kept switched off so as to prevent the terrorists from targeting them.

9. Suddenly, gunshots were heard from the house where all the senior officers were camping. Everybody ran helter-skelter and since the lights were off, some of them bumped into each other. When the firing stopped, panic stricken officers shouted for the lights to be switched on. Fortunately nobody received any injury. It was found that personal security officer of one of the Officers had accidentally pulled the trigger of his weapon.

10. Meanwhile the terrorists hiding inside the house kept firing at the security personnel at regular intervals. It was clear that the operation would not be over before sunset. The cordon of the target house was tightened and the area around the target house was kept illuminated to prevent the escape of terrorists while the lights of neighbouring buildings were switched off.

11. Fate of three missing policemen, the SDPO, SHO and the wireless operator of SP City, was still not clear. It was thought that they all could be alive but trapped inside the target house and therefore the police and the security forces should stop firing at the house and try and think of some means to get them out. It was clear by now that there was only one person firing at the forces and probably the second terrorist was dead or injured.

12. The SP City and the SSP of the district then took the owner of the house to one room and asked him about the actual facts and circumstances. The house owner informed that both the terrorists had been visiting his house for the past five to six days, stocking weapons, and had also done

a reconnaissance of the area. Both of them possessed one AK-47 each with at last five magazines full of ammunition. They had five grenades each besides some explosives and wireless sets. They were planning to attack the polytechnic camp where the Polling and Presiding Officers were collecting EVMs (electronic voting machines). They were very familiar with the owner who used to provide them food out of fear. They had also assured the owner that he and his family would not be harmed and that he would be compensated adequately after the task was complete.

13. Since the owner of the house knew the terrorists quite well, after talking to the SSP and SP City, in order to save his house from destruction, he proposed to go inside his house and talk to the terrorists hiding inside, to ask them to surrender.

14. The house owner thereafter went to the main door of his house and pleaded with the terrorist to come out and surrender. He requested them that his safety and that of his property would be jeopardized if they did not surrender. While the house owner and the terrorists were arguing with each other, the forces maintained strict fire control and observed with attention. During this time, to the surprise of the forces, all the three trapped policemen came to the balcony of the first floor and jumped out. The owner ran back seeing the policemen jumping out. The terrorists now started firing and the forces gave cover fire to the owner and to the three policemen to enable them escape.

15. The owner of the house reached back safely and informed the SSP that one terrorist was lying dead whereas the other was alive and had a weapon in his hand and a pouch having magazines inside. During the retaliatory firing by

the police and the security forces subsequently, the lone surviving terrorist made an attempt to climb on the roof and to jump to the adjacent house but got killed in the exchange of firing.

16. The house by now had caught fire. Fire tenders were called for help and they doused the fire. A thorough search of the house was carried out with the help of the bomb disposal squad who diffused the two IEDs (improvised explosive devices) which the terrorists had assembled. The police also recovered dead bodies of the two dead terrorists.

Analysis

1. No intelligence input should be taken lightly. Causalities happened in this operation because the police did not take the information very seriously in the first instance.
2. The contingent required for any operation should not be mixed too much. In this case three units of the CRPF, CISF and BSF along with two units of the police were involved in the operation which led to a lot of confusion.
3. In any situation, the officers should stick to the duties assigned to them. In this case it was not the duty of the SP City to search the bathroom outside the house without his PSOs who were carrying out the search inside the house. As a result, the PSO acted in haste and lost his life.
4. Actionable intelligence is mostly from a surprise source and rarely from an established source. This is evident from the fact that there were many inputs provided by the Intelligence agencies in the run up to the elections all of which were not verifiable and did not yield any result. It was the information of the CRPF Commandant who got it from a very casual source, led to the contact with the terrorists.

5. Nearby forces should always be informed to reduce confusion and to effectively coordinate the operation in case of an operation. However it is not necessary to involve everyone in the operation, for the purpose of maintaining clarity of command.
6. Any security force personnel entering in any building for search should be armed. In the present case the wireless operator and the SHO and the SDPO were unarmed. Once the firing started, these officers were trapped whereas those policemen, who were armed, saved themselves and escaped by firing.
7. Too many officers should not gather at one place. All the officers had gathered in a house close to the spot in this case. Another suicide attack during night hours by another group of terrorists could have been a possibility in this case.
8. Efforts should be made to finish the operation before sunset in order to avoid confusion and damages to civilians. Continuation of the operation in the night in this case led to complications.
9 In case of possibilities of continuation of operations during the night-time generator sets, wires, holders, bulbs, etc should be kept ready to light up the area as it is easy for a terrorist holed up in a house to escape taking advantage of darkness.
10. Bullet-proof vehicles should be kept ready as far as possible. This is more important in urban areas for moving close to the target area and also for any emergency evacuation. Bullet-proof vehicle came handy in this case in evacuating the injured Constable amidst heavy firing.
11. Efforts should be made to ascertain the exact situation inside the target house before planning the operation. The

number of terrorists, arms and ammunition with them, number of civilians inside, etc need to be ascertained.

12. During search, a locked door should be viewed with suspicion, especially when the owner makes an excuse to open the door. In this case, the statement of the owner that he was not well should have ringed alarm bells in the mind of the SP City.
13. Fire control should be exercised and coordination should be done with all the forces present before making any move. Everyone should be aware of the next move and should know who the chief planner is.
14. Fire service should be kept ready for any lengthy operation to reduce damages to the civilians. The fire department was quick to respond to the call in the present case although there was an extensive damage to the house due to fire.
15. A standby strength of policemen should be kept ready to handle law and order and to keep the media at a safe distance. In this case there was a big presence of national and international media at the site of the operation which was difficult to handle.

2. Ambush at a Remote Area in a Rural District

1. It was the month of June. The Superintendent of Police (SP) of the district thought of surprise visit to one of the remote police posts (PP) 'Y' in his area. The village where the police post was located was one of the last inhabited areas in the region. It was surrounded by forests on three sides which provided a 'safe haven' to the terrorists. The approach road to the police post was a long winding 'kuchha' road which had many recently constructed small culverts.

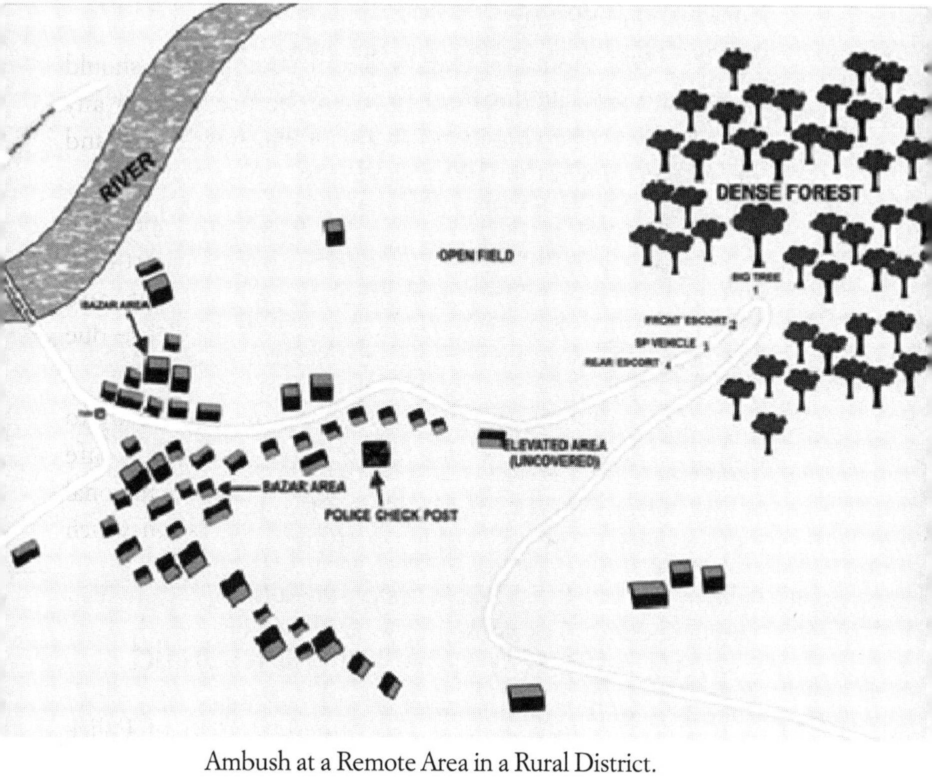

Ambush at a Remote Area in a Rural District.

2. On way to the police post, the SP stopped at a police station X (having jurisdiction over the police post). He interacted with the policemen of PS 'X', gave general instructions and then asked the SHO to accompany him to the PP. The SHO of the police station took to the driver's seat of the SP's vehicle. Because of his active participation in counter terrorism operation, the SHO was on the radar of the terrorists in the area.
3. In the convoy which moved from 'X' to 'Y', there were three Gypsies and sixteen police personnel in all including the drivers and the PSOs. All the policemen were equipped with AK-47 rifles and there was one LMG in the rear Gypsy. The SP preferred to move in a Gypsy instead of a heavy bullet proof car in order to save time and to gain more flexibility in movement in a hilly terrain. The road was broken at many places. At all such places the SP ordered his men to get down from the vehicle and check the culverts before crossing. The length of about twenty kilometres was covered in approximately two hours since all the culverts on way had to be crossed on foot first and had to be checked thoroughly for IEDs.
4. Convoy of the SP reached 'Y' safely at around 12:00 noon. The police post was housed in a hired building which was a wooden structure. It was located near the market and was quite vulnerable to attack by the terrorists. The idea of locating the police post near the Bazaar was to make it more accessible to the people and to gain intelligence.
5. The SP carried out a casual inspection of the police station. Except for terrorist related activities the crime figures were low. The registers were being maintained properly and a reward was given to the 'Munshi' of the police post for proper maintenance of records. This was basically an excuse to keep the policemen motivated in

their efforts at intelligence collection. The visiting team had 'Kahwa' (local hot drink) at the police post after which a worried in-charge PP requested the SP to come to his room for a confidential talk. When the SP moved to his room the in-charge PP informed him that there were more than 100 terrorists equipped with heavy arms in the area around the police post. The in-charge PP requested the SP to leave the area since the strength of the terrorists was much more than the strength of policemen with the SP. When the SP was talking to the in-charge PP, he saw from his window that the shutters of the shops in the Bazaar were coming down. This was a clear sign that terrorists had arrived and they were in good strength.

6. There were now two options with the SP. He could either ask for reinforcement from the Special Operations Group (SOG) and wait in the police post after taking position strategically, or move back for the time-being and then launch operation later with a bigger force. Waiting for the SOG would mean another three hours at least and very little time would be left to take on the terrorists before sunset. Moreover, holding on to a completely wooden structure with a limited number of sand bags was not a sensible idea. There were also chances of damages in the firing by the policemen themselves after the sunset and the whole situation could have become chaotic.

7. The SP decided to withdraw for the time being. He asked his men to get into the vehicles and prepare for the backward movement. The three vehicles were assembled and the convoy started to move back. The police party had travelled barely three hundred metres away from the police post when it started raining bullets. The front Gypsy was completely trapped in the firing. The middle Gypsy with the SP also received bullets on the radiator

and the front wind screen, and the vehicle came to a halt. The rear Gypsy was relatively safe. All the escort personnel jumped from it and started firing. The terrorists were using machine guns and grenades. It took some time to realize that fire was coming only from one side and the terrorists had taken position behind a huge 'deodar' (coniferous) tree (marked '1' in the map). The SP, the SHO and other PSOs had taken to the ground by that time. Policemen who had survived in the first vehicle had also taken to the ground. The wireless operator of the SP shouted on the wireless set to the In-charge PP to reach immediately or else provide covering fire for the SP to retreat. The In-charge PP replied that they had also been surrounded by the terrorists and they had to face heavy fire at the police post. The SP now realized that there was no scope of any external assistance and he had to manage with his own escort. The only hope was that the wireless headquarters of the district would have overheard the distress calls and dispatched a police team on their own.

8. The firing from the side of the terrorists continued for about fifteen minutes and then stopped. The SP shouted to his men to stop firing. He then signalled the policemen in the rear Gypsy to fan out and clear both the sides first. His escort personnel moved out and secured both the sides. Then, some PSOs of the SP were asked to approach the site from where the firing had originated. The PSOs took help of cover fire by the rear escort and approached the site. It was found that the terrorists had fled leaving behind some ammunition. Some fruits (oranges and banana) were also found at that place.

9. It was now time to take stock of the losses since the place was secured from all sides. There was one policeman dead

in the front escort. One policeman in the SP's vehicle had received bullet injury on his hand and was bleeding profusely. The injured policeman was immediately shifted in the rear Gypsy, the only vehicle in running condition. Although there was always a risk of another attack, the injured had to be shifted for medical attention. The SP called the in-charge of the police post (IC PP). Since firing had stopped on the police post, the in-charge managed to reach the spot. He was asked to shift the dead bodies to the district headquarters and also to start the legal formalities. The SP then briefed his men to go into the forests nearby in search for the attackers. When he asked his men to count their ammunition, he was surprised to know that there were only twenty rounds of ammunition left of AK-47 and fifteen rounds of LMG. The SP himself had twenty-three rounds of AK ammunition in his single magazine which he was carrying. With this kind of fire-power left, there was no point to search the terrorists.

10. The SP called for reinforcement from the nearby security forces since the police party was left with very little ammunition to take on another ambush. The reinforcements arrived after about two hours as the reinforcement convoy had to go through the same drills of culvert clearance by foot and negotiating ambush points by dominating the height.

11. A week later, a combined team of the police and other security forces cordoned off the entire 50 sq km area of the jungle adjoining the police post and carried out a search operation. Terrorists were taken by surprise and the top most commander of the terrorists operating in the area got killed along with two of his associates. A large quantity of arms and ammunition was also recovered during this operation.

Analysis

1. Signs of trouble should always be carefully noticed. In this case the shopkeepers downed the shutter on the arrival of terrorists. This was a clear indication that something was going to happen which was not in the interest of the shopkeepers. The SP could sense this sign in the present case.
2. While moving for an operation in a terrorist affected hilly area, culverts should be physically checked before crossing it, especially on a 'kuccha' track.
3. During movement a reasonable gap between all the vehicles of the convoy should be maintained. In this case because of the gap, while the first vehicle was completely trapped in the fire and the middle vehicle of the SP received a partial hit, the third vehicle of the convoy could escape unhurt in the ambush and was able to retaliate when attacked by the terrorists.
4. In case of an ambush on a plain straight road, the standard practice is to speed away as far as possible. In case of an ambush on a hilly road and especially in a situation like this where there is a sharp uphill bend, one should leave the vehicle and take to the ground immediately when the vehicles get stuck in an ambush. There could have been more casualties had everyone not left the vehicle and taken to the ground.
5. Vehicles should not be used for movement when threat is imminent. In this case during the backward movement from the police post, the police party should have walked on foot especially when they realized about the presence of terrorists. It was easy to move some distance on foot clearing the area slowly and then use the vehicle.
6. When proceeding to an operational area, care should be taken to avoid stopping at any place other than the final

destination. This can lead to leakage of information regarding movement of security forces. In the present situation information had been leaked from the police station at 'X' and the terrorists had enough time to prepare for the ambush.

7. There should be proper fire control during an ambush like situation. In this case had the terrorists come down to the convoy after the initial firing, they could have captured policemen alive since very little ammunition was left with the police party. It was found that during the ambush the escort personnel panicked and fired indiscriminately seeing their fellow colleagues injured and dead.

3. Operation Involving a Religious Place

1. In this case information was received from a reliable source that some terrorists were hiding at a village. The district SP consulted his SP (Operations) and an operation was planned. The plan was shared with the local unit of CPMF (Central Paramilitary Forces) battalion (which was stationed there to assist in counter terrorism duties) who agreed to pool in the troops for the operation. The Commandant of the CPMF mustered two columns of troops. The SOG of the police had thirty men ready for the operation. A cordon was laid at night around the entire village. Announcement was made from loudspeakers at the mosque asking every male member of the village to come out and assemble near the mosque so as to carry out search of all the houses.
2. While the cordon was being laid, firing suddenly started from inside a house. Since it was still dark, there was total confusion among the troops regarding the exact origin of the firing. It was also not clear whether the firing was by the terrorists or by our own troops. It was fortunate that

the Commandant and the SP (Operations) were on the spot while the cordon was being laid. The cordon had been well planned and the areas to be covered by the SOG and the CPMF were clearly demarcated and there was a system to identify the intersection between the troops to avoid any confusion. Both the commanders immediately passed the information on the wireless set to keep the cordon tight and not allow anyone to escape. The process of assembling the villagers at the mosque was put on hold till the first light. The troops followed the directions and the cordon was strengthened. The five search parties which were to carry out the search also joined the cordon to strengthen it since it was by now certain that the terrorists were inside the village which had about 200 houses.

3. The troops waited for the first light and both the commanders first took a round of the village to see the cordon. The entire process took half an hour. When they were satisfied that the cordon had not been breached, the search teams were now taken out again from the cordon and briefed about the search process. One group set out for the mosque to make announcement to the villagers to come out and facilitate search of their houses. As soon as the team reached near the mosque, they were greeted by a volley of bullets. They immediately took cover and replied the fire. The SP (Operation) was now joined by the district SP who had reached the spot hearing about the firing at night. Two cordons were now made, one around the mosque and the other around the village. While the team around the mosque took on the terrorists inside the mosque, other teams carried out the search of the rest of the village. All the male members of the village were made to sit in an open ground at a safe place and the source also sat in the same group to identify if there was any terrorist among

them. As and when their houses were searched the villagers were asked to accompany the search party. The search of the rest of the village was completed in about three hours' time.

4. It was 10.30 AM by now and everyone was confident that there were only two terrorists in the village and both of them were inside the mosque. One of the terrorists was the district commander of a terrorist outfit. It was also ascertained that there was no civilian in the mosque. The outer cordon of the village was kept in position and all the officers concentrated on the main target area of the mosque. Firing was intermittent from the mosque. It was clear that there was an attempt to save ammunition on the part of the terrorists. The troops in order to protect sanctity of the mosque appealed to the terrorists to come out of the mosque and surrender. The terrorists however, did not pay heed to the appeal by the policemen. The local Maulvi was also requested to appeal to the terrorists but his requests were also ignored. Some Ikhwaan (surrendered terrorists) members who were among the SOG also tried to argue with the terrorists in the local language but this also did not bring any result. It was clear after interaction with the locals that both the terrorists were foreigners and there was no point making any appeals to them to surrender.

5. It was 12 PM by this time and the commanders decided to rotate the troops to give them a break in groups of ten, to allow them to take their breakfast. The villagers were also left in small batches to take care of their families and to take their food. The Commandant arranged a doctor from his battalion to take care of the medical needs of the villagers and also to take care of any casualties during the operation. Instruction was given at the battalion headquarters to make

packed food for the night in case the operation continued for the night. Arrangement for generators to light up the target area at night was also done. The district SP asked for tear gas ammunition at the site to be used in case of need. Both stun grenades and tear smoke grenades were brought.

6. After making no headway till 1400 hours, the commandos of the SOG made an attempt to storm inside the mosque but were greeted by heavy firing from inside. One commando who had a peep inside the mosque in the process stated that both the terrorists were couched in the depression in the centre of the mosque along the rear wall which was meant for the prayers. It was then decided to use tear gas shells to make them come out of the mosque. The same was used by firing tear gas grenades from the window. The sound of coughing by the terrorists could be heard from inside but the troops were finding it equally difficult to see and it was not possible for anyone to enter the mosque without a mask under the circumstances. The terrorists did not come out of the mosque despite repeated rounds of tear gas use.

7. The commanders on the spot now gathered to decide the further course of action. It was 1300 hours by this time and the security forces had a limited time before it became dark. It was collectively decided to make an attempt of storming inside by a joint team of the CPMF and the SOG. It was planned that while the covering fire would be done from the side window, the commandos would enter from the main door. The plan was started but as soon as the first team entered, they were greeted by heavy fire from inside. One CPMF jawan received grievous injuries and had to be immediately evacuated. The entire squad which had stormed inside was now engaged in the rescue of the

trapped jawan. Seeing this second attempt also fail, it was decided that there was no point storming from the front door since the terrorists were having a pot shot at the forces from their hiding position.

8. A final attempt was made by the help of a bullet-proof police vehicle. The idea was to take the vehicle with well-armed SOG members in reverse gear and to place it in front of the main door. The SOG would then use the small hole in the rear door to target the terrorists. Destiny was however, not on the side of the police that day. The terrorists fired on the bullet proof vehicle. One bullet came in through the space between the rear door and the side hinges, ricocheted through the side steel sheet and hit the driver of the vehicle from behind. The driver barely managed to take the vehicle out before succumbing to his injuries.
9. The security forces now had two hours left before it became dark. By this time messages had been sent to the Police Headquarters and to the higher formations of CPMF about the terrorists inside the mosque who directed to follow maximum restraint.
10. The troops were now getting tired. The loss of two men, one from the police and the other from the CPMF added to the agony. The terrorists inside the mosque were successful in holding out against a hundred policemen for ten hours now. It was now conveyed from the higher headquarters that there had to be no firing of rocket launchers on the mosque. The CPMF units were asked to wait for further orders. At 7 PM, orders came from the higher authorities of CPMF that they should leave the spot and the matter should be dealt by the local police in view of the sensitivity of the situation of militants inside a mosque.

11. The police was caught in a strange situation when the CPMF left. A different strategy was now thought by the SP (Operations). It was decided that the police will also withdraw for the moment. The source who was among the villagers and whose identity was known to the SP (Operations) only, would be called among a group of villagers for questioning. During questioning, the source would be tasked to keep a track of the terrorists after the withdrawal of the force. The source would pose as a well-wisher and would be the first to reach the terrorists after the withdrawal of troops. He was paid to take care of the medical and other needs of the terrorists. He was also advised to take the terrorists to his own house for a 'Dawat' (a treat for giving a tough fight to the forces and forcing them to flee). Their next task was to win over their confidence and to keep a track of them. He was specifically asked to be patient and not provide the information in a hurry. He was asked to wait for the ideal opportunity so that they could be taken by surprise.
12. The opportune moment came faster than expected. Within a week, another information was provided about the presence of the same two terrorists in another village. The source had informed that there was a wedding party which was attended by them and they were deep asleep in a house after a heavy lunch in the afternoon. The SP informed the same Commandant of the CPMF and launched an operation with the SOG men to take on the terrorists. The terrorists were not lucky this time.

Analysis

1. In an operation it must be ensured that the cordon of the area is tight and each party has communication with the other, whether physically or through wireless set. Effective

cordon in this case prevented the terrorists from escaping at night.

2. Search of an area should not be conducted while it is dark. One must wait for the first light. Had the search been started at night, there would have been a lot of confusion in maintaining the liaison between the search groups. Any firing from any other side, or even accidentally by the security forces, would have led to commotion.
3. In an operation, there is a possibility of the terrorist trying to leave his weapon and camouflage himself with the local people. In such a situation it is a good idea to keep the local source present with the locals so that such a person can be identified.
4. In case an operation continues for a long time, needs of the local people, especially medical and food must be taken care of.
5. In a long drawn operation proper rotation of troops and arrangement of food for the men should be made.
6. The operation party should be properly equipped for room intervention with stun grenades, tear smoke, gas masks etc. In this case the use of tear smoke definitely limited the scope of retaliation by the terrorists. However, lack of proper masks with the police also put a handicap on their capabilities.

4. Operation in a Remote Hilly Area

1. In the winter month of December, the SDPO (Sub-Divisional Police Officer) of a Sub-Division got a source information regarding presence of a group of armed terrorists in a rural village 'X' of his sub-division in the border district with a neighbouring country. The information mentioned

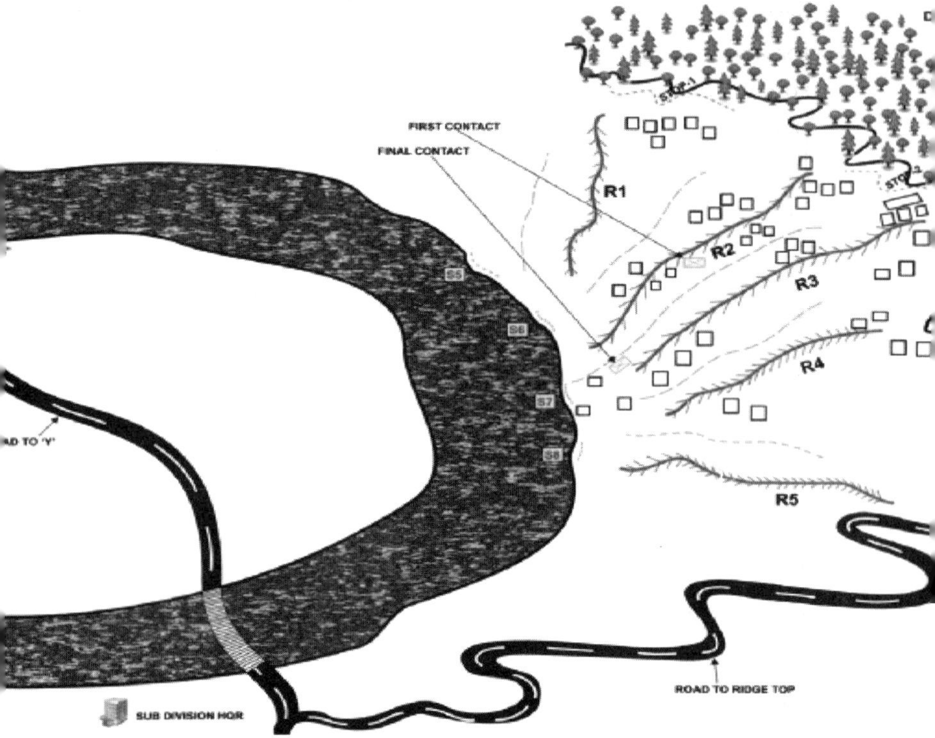

Encounter in a Rural Area.

about presence of the terrorists in the general area and no specific house was mentioned by the source. However, the information revealed that the terrorists were planning to spend the night in the village.

2. The SDPO discussed the information with the IRP (Indian Reserve Police) Battalion officers, stationed there for counter terrorism duties. A map of the area was immediately called for and the officers discussed the plan. The terrain and the spread of the village required availability of at least 200 personnel to cordon off the area. The IRP commandant had two companies (effective strength of 100 men for operation duties) available with him. The SDPO agreed to muster 50 police personnel from the strength of the Special Operations Group (SOG) and from the police station staff of the local police station. Rest of the police component was requisitioned from the district headquarters. The village 'X' fell under the jurisdiction of police station 'Y' where a component of IRP was also present for protection of minorities and for counter terrorism duties. The SDPO decided that for reasons of maintaining secrecy of the information and for maintaining surprise factor, the local police station would not be informed about the operation till the full cordon was in place and the search started.
3. There were five ridge lines running through the village. Each ridge line had to be manned by security forces all along the length. It was decided that once the ridge lines were manned and stops were in place for preventing escape of the terrorists, the search parties would begin house to house search to look for the hiding terrorists.
4. Police Components from the district headquarters arrived at 'X' in the evening, comprising of one Inspector, two Sub-Inspectors and other constabulary. The local SOG

team comprised of one DySP, one Inspector and two Sub-Inspectors besides other constabulary. The IRP strength included one Deputy Commandant, two Assistant Commandants and other personnel. Teams were divided into five teams for five ridges, four teams for stops between the ridge lines and another four teams for stops on the lower side. Besides these teams, there had to be at least five teams for carrying out the search. The teams therefore had to have eighteen team leaders and at least thirteen guides well-versed with the area who could place the teams as per the deployment plan. The team leaders and the guides therefore had to be informed of the plan of action well in advance and care had to be taken to ensure that the information did not get leaked. This was a difficult problem as the guides were locals of the area having their family members in the village and hence vulnerable to retaliation by the terrorists. The guides therefore needed to be camouflaged with other security force personnel and hence were dressed in police uniform.

5. The SDPO divided his team into eighteen parts, each headed by an officer at least of the rank of a Sub-Inspector. He pulled out thirteen guides for the area from the SOG who had operated extensively in the area of 'X'. It was also ensured that the local police personnel of that area were sent for operation in other areas on general information. A briefing session was conducted at 10 PM at night. The troops were made to fall in at that time to ensure that the chance of leaking of information was minimized. Two briefing sessions took place. One session was with the entire strength of the police personnel which was being launched for operation while the other briefing was specifically for the team leaders and the guides who were to take part in the operation. This was different from

the traditional briefing pattern of the security forces where all the personnel were briefed together. In the first briefing, general information was given to everyone regarding the presence of the terrorists. The plan was told regarding formation of teams for ridge lines, stops and search parties. They were briefed regarding precautions to be taken at the time of search and about the reaction of the teams in the situation of an exchange of firing with the terrorists. General briefing regarding movement at night, distance to be maintained between two police personnel, no use of torch light, etc was done. Care was taken not to tell the area of operation to the troops. It was informed that the team leaders would be told about the area and the exact plan and the troops would obey orders of their team leaders. The second briefing was done for the eighteen team leaders and the thirteen guides regarding the deployment plan, the timing of deployment and the methodology of communication between the parties. Care was taken to ensure that there was some communication between each party either directly or through the control station. A location was therefore also selected in that area where a control station would be set up with a base station wireless set from where all the parties could be contacted. Sufficient number of hand-held wireless sets with spare batteries was supplied to the teams. Briefing was also done regarding the reaction of each team in case of a face-off with terrorists in any particular area. The teams had to be told about the transport arrangement of the troops to the general area and how the movement of the vehicles would take place. It was ensured that the vehicles would be parked at a place which was not directly visible from the village. This was done as the terrorists were known to have a very good network of information in their area of operation, to alert them about any vehicular movement in their area, especially late at night or early morning. It was also planned that there would be visible movement of dummy vehicles in some other direction late at night to mislead the hiding terrorists. It was decided that the vehicles for the operation would move slowly without their headlights on, and would be parked at a place far away from the original disembarking point. This in turn required that the troops had to move long distances on foot to reach their deployment area. Since it was winter time, this was not much of a problem for the troops. Advance planning for supply of packed food to the troops from the IRP headquarters was made in case the operation continued for long hours.

6. After the briefing, the team leaders as well as the guides were sent to IRP camps for stay at night till the operation was launched. This was done to ensure absolute secrecy regarding the operation being launched. At 2 o'clock in the night, all the troops were made to fall in and this time a combined briefing of the troops as well as of team leaders and guides was done. At this point of time the complete briefing regarding the area of operations, the type of information available, the mode of conduct of operations, precautions to be taken and post-operation movement was explained to the troops in detail. Vehicles were lined up for the transportation of troops to the area sufficiently away from the site of the operation. The vehicles were made to move with a gap of at least 100 metres. Care was taken not to transport the entire group of 200 men from the same route and at the same time precautions were taken not to overcrowd any vehicle in order to prevent any casualty arising out of an ambush or IED blasts by the terrorists on the way. Troops were dispatched from three directions to ensure maintaining surprise in the operation.

7. By 3.30 AM, all the police parties had reached their respective advance staging area from where they had to travel on foot. After reaching a particular pre-decided place the troops were divided into various sub-groups according to the earlier plan and then asked to move to the respective places along with team leaders and guides. During this deployment and movement on foot, usual standard practices such as maintenance of distance between two persons, method of carrying arms and movement without help of the light were followed. The use of night vision devices by the scouts was done in areas where the risk factor was very high.
8. By 4.30 AM, well before first light, all the policemen were in position at their respective places. The team leaders conveyed information on wireless station to the base monitoring station that they had reached the designated places and the troops had been deployed. The base station in turn informed the SDPO and the Commandant through wireless set regarding deployment of security forces. It had been earlier decided that the Commandant of IRP would be accompanying the troops from the base of hills and the SDPO would be accompanying the search party from the top of the hill. Search had to be carried out from the top towards bottom as was the practice of the cordon and search operation in the hill areas. After receiving information that the troops had been deployed, the SDPO waited for the first light to launch search operation between various ridge-lines which had been manned by the security forces. Care was taken not to allow movement in or out of the cordon.
9. The search operations started at 5.30 AM in the morning when all the four search teams started searching houses one by one from the top towards the bottom of the

hill. Usual hiding areas such as cowsheds, store areas, dummy walls, cupboards, kitchen areas and toilets were specifically searched. At around 10 AM, when the troops had searched most of their respective areas and were getting tired, suddenly there was a burst of fire from a house on the police personnel of team 2. All the team members of team 2, comprising of one SI, one ASI and 12 jawans rushed towards the area from where the fire was coming. The terrorists hiding inside the house immediately came out and started firing at the searching party. They were retreating towards the downhill side, firing back at the searching party at the same time. Hearing the shots of gunfire in the adjacent area, members of team 1 left their search areas and ran towards the team 2 area violating the instructions given by the SDPO and the Commandant. Direction of their movement was not known to team 2 members although the leader of team 1 tried to contact the leader of team 2 on the wireless set. It was observed that since the firing had started, everyone was trying to collect some information on the wireless set regarding what was happening. As a result, the wireless network got jammed and communication could not take place between different parties. The SDPO instructed the base station to give a general call to all the team members and ask them not to use the wireless set unless asked for. Due to the jamming of wireless sets team 1 and team 2 could not coordinate properly and it was found that both the teams were approaching the target area from the same side. The firing continued for some time. The militants also lobbed grenades on the search parties. Within 10 minutes of firing, a wireless message was received from team 2 that one of the police personnel of their team had received bullet injuries. It was also intimated by the team that the terrorists were three in number and had taken shelter inside a semi-'pucca' house in the nearby area and were firing continuously on the search parties. The SDPO immediately asked the search parties to cordon the house and take proper cover. Team 1 members were also by now in touch with team 2 members and joined with the team 1 to cordon the house and retaliate firing by the terrorists. The injured constable was evacuated from the site but succumbed to injuries while being taken to the hospital. By now, the target area was clear and the SDPO along with his personal security officers reached the place where the terrorists were hiding. The other search teams apart from team 1 were asked to carry out search operation in their respective areas. The reserve team with the SDPO was asked to take care of the area left by the team 1. By this time, the Commandant of IRP also arrived from the foothills side and zeroed on the house where the terrorists were hiding.

10. Since the police parties were in a commanding position and time was on their side, the SDPO used a loudspeaker to ask the hiding terrorists to surrender. The terrorists however refused to surrender and instead fired back to show their intention. The SDPO then tried to use tear gas inside the house but it was not effective since there was a strong wind blowing in the area. Absence of proper windows in a kuccha house made the tear gas even more ineffective. Since house intervention was risky in this situation, it was decided to use rocket launchers at the target house in retaliation to the fire coming from the terrorists. This action was extremely risky since the house had been cordoned from all the four sides and in case the rocket missed the target area, there was a great likelihood that the police party on the other side of the cordon would receive splinter injuries. The SDPO and

the IRP Commandant therefore got together and decided to use rocket launchers after clearing the firing line. After two rockets were fired, one of the terrorists ran out of the house downhill side, firing on the police party, but got killed in the exchange of firing. There were now two more terrorists left inside and the house had by now caught fire. Information was immediately provided to the SHO of the local police station to get a magistrate on the spot.

11. The operation continued for two hours. The terrorists holed up inside were using their ammunition carefully, conserving the same, perhaps waiting for the night. The fire was spreading to other rooms very slowly. Since the area was not approachable by road, no fire tenders could reach the spot. It was now more than 12 hours since the launch of the operation. Food was therefore arranged for the police party as decided earlier. The reserve strength for the operation was utilized for giving a break to the troops for having food. One team was provided food at a time to ensure that the cordon was intact. Since the search of other areas was also complete, the locals were allowed to move out of the cordon after proper verification with the help of a 'source'.

12. It was now getting late. Only one hour was left before it became dark. By this time more than half of the house had caught fire. It was evident that the terrorists had moved to the rooms which had not caught fire. However no shots were now being fired from inside. The police personnel were getting tired. It was decided that a team will now be sent to the rooms which had not caught fire, to search the house. A SOG team stormed the house and ten minutes later informed that they found dead body of a slain terrorist lying inside the house and an AK-47 rifle.

They said that they could not find the body of any other terrorist. It was now assumed that the remaining terrorists had most probably died in the fire which had spread inside the house.

13. The operation was now over. All the officers started congratulating each other. A team was sent inside again to look for any arms and ammunition which was left over. Soon after the team went inside, firing started again. There was mayhem outside. All the officers and men ran to the nearest possible cover. The SDPO and the Commandant now took control and ensured that the cordon around the house was again in place. The search party which had been sent inside had also come out to make themselves secure. The team leader informed that one terrorist was hiding inside the huge grain box. As soon as the search party went inside and started searching the huge box for arms, the terrorist hiding inside started firing. Since he could not see anyone, there were no casualties on the side of the police. It was now not certain whether the terrorist was still inside the grain box or had come out. Since it had become dark by now, there was no option but to wait outside for the entire night. The SDPO closed in the cordon and made a rotation pattern for the troops to spend the night. Lighting arrangements were made outside with focus at the house.

14. The troops waited for the night firing intermittently to convey a message that the cordon outside was intact and the troops were alert. Early morning after the first light the SOG team stormed inside and took the last surviving terrorist by surprise who got killed in the exchange of firing. Another AK-47 rifle was recovered from the house. The operation was now over. The troops were asked to

move back in the same manner in which they had come to the operation site. Since it was day time now and since the ROP parties were in place, the vehicles could now move back from one route safely. A debriefing session was conducted to tell the troops about the mistakes committed during the operation. The local SHO was asked to take care of the scene of crime and to conduct the investigation besides conducting procedural formalities.

Analysis

1. All information provided by the source should be taken with the same seriousness. In this case the information was not specific. Hence a large area had to be cordoned and a lot of effort was to be put to muster the strength required for the operation.
2. It is always better to involve the local police personnel in any operation since they have better knowledge of the area.
3. A map or a sand model should be used to plan the operation, especially in a hilly area. The requirement of troops for the operation can only be gauged after looking at the map and after taking into consideration the contours of the area.
4. Every sub-team should have a team leader who should be equipped with communication system. Also, a local guide should be kept with each team.
5. Sufficient night vision devices should be kept for the team if possible. This becomes necessary for all the operations which have to be conducted at night.
6. All men should be briefed before the operation. Details of the operation can be discussed with a core team who

should not be allowed to communicate with anyone or to move outside the camp after being told about the operation. Giving the details of the information to the entire team well in advance can lead to the information being compromised, especially when a large number of troops are locals.

7. Vehicles must be kept sufficiently away from the actual place of operation. Further, the vehicles should not move with the lights on during any movement at night near the operation area. Sufficient distance should be maintained between the vehicles. Some vehicles should preferably be sent from a different route.
8. Sending dummy vehicles to areas away from the operational area can be useful to mislead the terrorists. Their sources keep them informed about the movement of security forces. In this case dummy vehicles were moved in opposite direction to mislead the terrorists.
9. While moving on foot, a safe distance between the police personnel should be maintained. This helps in minimizing casualties in case of an ambush.
10. As far as possible, the local Magistrate must be informed about the operation after a contact with the terrorists has been established. The information provided to the Magistrate should be properly documented.
11. The leader of the operation should never declare any area as 'clear' before he gets complete details about the operation site. In this case, premature celebration could have led to more casualties on the police side.
12. Debriefing of the troops is a must to make them aware of their mistakes. Although after a long operation the troops are tired, they should not be left without debriefing.

5. Operation Near the City in a Hilly Area

1. It was a bright sunny morning in the still chilly month of March. Sitting on the terrace of his office, the SP of the district observed an old man, known for providing frivolous information to get access to senior officers of the police and other forces, arguing with the sentries at the gate to come inside. The SP thought for a second and then signalled his sentries to allow the person to meet him. The old man gave the SP a big smile from the gate and came inside.
2. There were many people lined up to meet the SP with their grievances and the SP was meeting them according to their turn in the queue. The source was located at the end of a long queue. While the wait was on, he paced to and fro and was clearly getting impatient. After waiting for five minutes, he walked up to the Personal Assistant (PA) of the SP and said in a hushed note that he needed to speak to the SP urgently. The PA could sense that he was an informant and had come up with some information. Informants were always given a priority in this terrorist infested district. When the PA sent the message to the SP, he was initially sceptical since he knew the poor credentials of the source. However he allowed him to come to him.
3. The source approached the SP with a smile on the face which conveyed that this time there was more weight in the information which he was providing. His demeanour reflected the sense of fear inside him. The SP greeted him and offered a cup of tea and asked what brought him there. He immediately came down to business and said in a hushed tone that there were three terrorists inside his house. The SP realised immediately that the credibility of the information was very high since this time it was

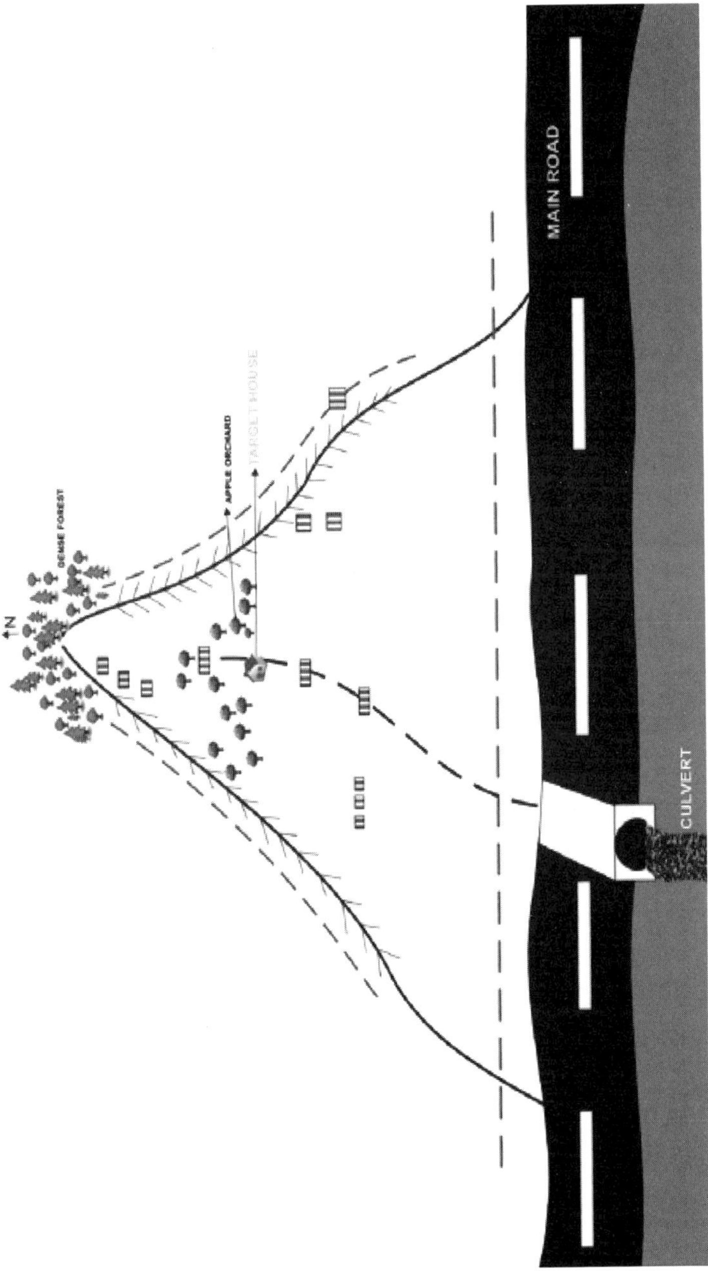

Operation near the City.

about his own house. He had never come up with such information before. He went on to give the details of the information. The three terrorists were senior commanders who had completed their tenure of stay in the area and were on their way out. They did not have a local guide with them who could liaise with the locals and make their exit safe and secure. He also informed that the terrorists had travelled the whole night from a nearby mountain top to reach his house. They reached at the early hours of the day and had asked him to prepare food for them. After having food, all of them had gone off to sleep. He informed that their plan was to start moving out before the first light the next day. They had asked him to accompany them to the border as a guide.

4. The SP immediately realised the urgency of the situation. He had seven hours to plan and complete the operation. He had time to plan the operation since it was known that the terrorists did not know their way out and were fast asleep after having travelled for the whole night. The SP instructed all his men at the headquarters to prepare for the operation. The DySP (Operations), DySP (DAR) (in-charge of the armed reserve in police lines) and the local SHO were asked to be ready for the operation. The DySP (Headquarters) who had a vast experience in counter-terrorism operations was not available since he had just returned from a night-long operation and was resting. The SP despatched a team of five police personnel, well-armed and in civil clothes, to the village to keep an eye on the house of the source so that any movement of the terrorists from that house could be tracked. A total of fifty police personnel were arranged within an hour. A short briefing session was held in the district police lines and the team commanders were briefed about the information. They were asked to prepare a select

group of seven police personnel for room intervention. The district police had recently acquired rocket launchers, provided by the police headquarters. The SP asked the DySP (DAR) to keep a contingent ready with the rocket launchers which could prove to be handy in case the terrorists got holed up inside the house without any civilian with them.

5. The target village was situated barely 6 kilometres from the town. House of the source was located at a height which was a thirty minute trek from the road head. One team of the Special Operations Group of the police was despatched to cover the house from the top of the ridge line. The house was surrounded by two parallel ridge lines from the eastern and western sides. Two strong teams of fifteen men each were asked to cover the house from the east and the west. An extra component taken out from the police station was asked to put up stops from the south side with the local SHO as the commander. The SP placed himself at a vantage point on the eastern ridge and placed two contingents with light machine guns pointed towards the two doors opening outside. This was to take care of anyone moving out from the main door. The DySP (Operations) was tasked to approach the house with the rocket launcher contingent. Announcement was made on a loud hailer asking the terrorist to surrender but there was no response from the house. The SP took permission from the house owner to use rocket launchers on the house with a promise of suitable compensation. The house owner agreed to do so. He was in fact more than eager that this takes place since this would send a signal to the terrorists that he was a victim and not a benefactor. The DySP (DAR) was told to position himself north of the house to prevent any chances of escape from that side.

6. House intervention in this situation could have been risky. Therefore, after the cordon was laid and each party had communicated regarding their positions, the SP decided to fire a rocket at the outer wall of the house in order to take the terrorists by surprise. Before doing that, it was ensured that the LMGs were in position at each and every possible exit route so that any armed man exiting from the house could be taken on.
7. The first round of rocket launcher (RL) fire went off and hit the outer wall but nothing happened. Another round was fired but this time it did not hit the target and instead exploded very close to the place where the DySP DAR had positioned himself. Luckily, no one was injured. This prompted the SP to ask the RL party to move closer to the house so that it did not miss the target. The RL party moved closer to the target and it was now barely 30 metres from the target. The RL was loaded again and fired. This time again it hit the outer wall but was not able to make any significant impact. At this point of time, probably hearing the wireless conversation of the SP on the set, the local CRPF Commandant came on the wireless and advised that the RL should be moved back to a certain distance so that the rocket is properly charged to explode. It was clear that the person handling the RL was not trained enough to know the nuances of handling a sensitive weapon like that. Had the main handler present on the spot, probably this problem would not have arisen.
8. The RL contingent was again moved back and a rocket was fired. This time the rocket exploded with a thundering sound and shook the outer wall of the house. This time one terrorist tried to move out of the house, firing on the police party from his Kalashnikov, but got killed in the exchange of fire with the alert policeman with LMG who

was concentrating at the exit door. Rest of the two terrorists by now had also started firing on the police party from the window. All the police personnel were positioned with a suitable cover. The SP, however again alerted all men to take cover so that no unnecessary casualty took place. He also spoke to the contingent commanders to exercise a strict fire control so that they focus on the available target and do not fire aimlessly which could injure the policemen on the other side.

9. By this time the firing had intensified and the terrorists were firing heavily. The SP signalled his RL party to fire another rocket launcher at the target house. Another thunderous sound occurred. This time the rocket went inside from the main door and exploded inside. The terrorists hiding inside probably thought that the house would now be destroyed. They ran out firing from their weapons and took position in the fields outside the house. They however had no cover to protect them except small apple trees which could not protect them for too long. The two remaining terrorists got killed in exchange of firing with the police party after a ten minutes battle. There were no casualties on the police side. It was one of the cleanest operations carried out by the police in the recent times. The entire operation was over within two hours of cordon of the area.

10. On search of the belongings of the killed terrorists, three AK-56 rifles and twelve magazines along with some grenades and ammunition were recovered. Some matrix sheets were recovered using which the terrorists were communicating in coded language. Some documents were also recovered which showed distribution of money to the terrorists operating in the area. Some identity cards were also recovered which showed that all the three persons were

non-locals. The house of the informant was also searched but nothing significant could be found.

11. It was now the time to withdraw. While withdrawing from the place, the SP instructed that the house owner be apprehended in full public view and questioned aggressively. He was detained later at the police station on his own request. A police party was kept stationed near his house for three days so that any terrorist reaching that place to enquire about the death of their colleagues could be trapped. The terrorists however did not arrive. The source was later released and a suitable compensation was given to him for the damage to his house due to RL fire. The matrix sheets recovered from the possession of the terrorists was immediately provided to the police telecom division which was monitoring intercepts. It was also used by the district wireless monitoring cell to decode the intercepted messages. This however did not last very long since the operatives of the concerned terrorist outfit got the news of the killing of their cadres and immediately went for revision of their matrix codes. The document related to distribution of funds to the terrorists operating in the area was investigated by the Special investigation team of the district and on that basis, a number of over ground workers working for the terrorists were apprehended.

Analysis

1. Entire story of the 'source' should be listened. It helps in proper planning and execution of the operation. In this case, the fact that the terrorists did not have a guide with them, coupled with the fact that they were tired and sleeping, made planning of the operation easier.
2. Room interventions are risky and the chances of casualty of the security force personnel entering a house generally remain

very high. It is always better to use some other means to get the terrorists out of the house in which they have taken shelter and then to take them on. In this case, the rocket launchers proved very effective to compel the terrorists to move out of the house.

3. Seizures made from the site of operation should be carefully analysed as these can lead to some valuable information, especially regarding the over ground workers and associates of the terrorists involved in the incident.

6. 'Fidayeen' Attack at Police Housing Colony

1. Towards the end of the summer season in the capital city, by around 7 PM, the Civil Secretariat had closed down. The employees were returning to their homes after the day's work in the office. The sun had set and it was dark. Electricity supply in the city was not very regular and power shut down was common. The police housing colony located on the outskirts of the city was beaming with activity.
2. It was the month of Ramadan and the police families were busy with 'Iftaar'. The police colony had a boundary wall all around, with two sentries manning the front and back side of the colony round the clock. Usually at this time during 'Iftaar', the police sentries also used to take some time off for their evening food. Vehicles belonging to the police personnel were known to the sentries and they could make out about the owner of the vehicle at one look. On that day, the power had gone off and the sentries were with their guards down on the main gate. Suddenly there was a grenade explosion on the main gate. The sentry who had come out of his bunker received injuries and died on the spot. Two 'fidayeen' attackers (suicide attackers)

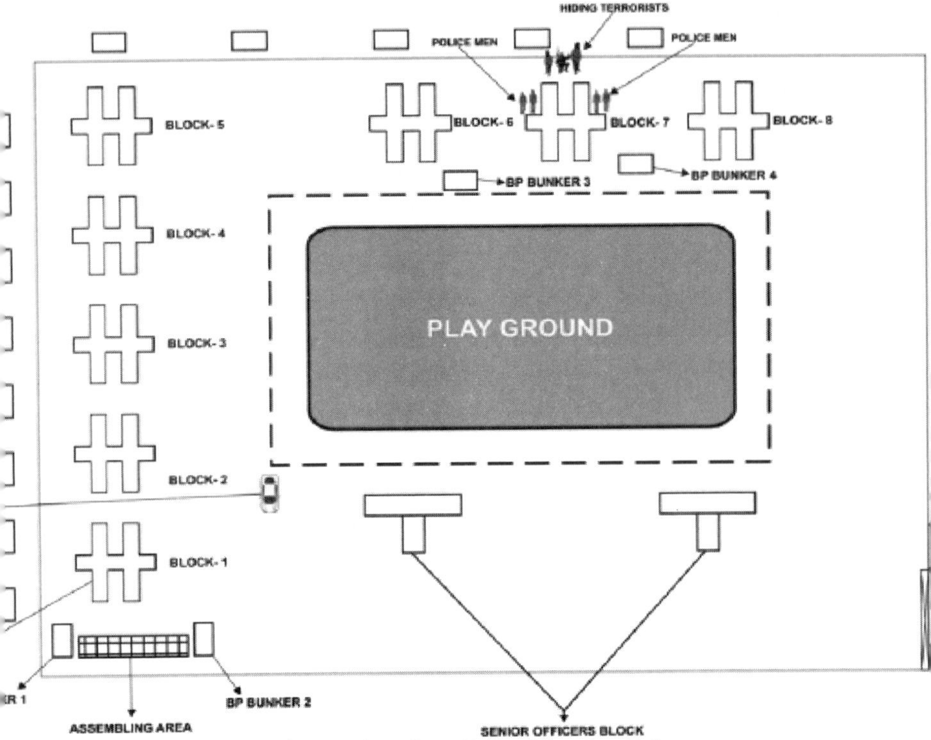

Fidayeen Attack on Police Housing Colony.

armed with Kalashnikov rifles and wearing police uniforms soon came inside. They fired at the sentry and moved inside the police colony firing on anyone within sight. Two persons belonging to the police families died in the firing. There was total commotion inside the police colony. Rest of the guard personnel hurriedly went to their bunkers and took control of the entry and exit of the colony. Immediate result of this move was that the 'fidayeen' attackers got confined inside the colony and could not move out.

3. A wireless message was flashed immediately by the guard on duty that there was an attack by terrorists who had sneaked inside the police colony. The Senior Superintendent of Police (SSP) immediately rushed to the colony. It was the jurisdiction of the SP City (North) who also rushed in with his escort. The SP (Operations) who was in-charge of all operations in the city also started moving towards the police colony with his escort. The SP (South) and the SDPO of civil secretariat (CS) area who were supervising security arrangements during movement of the Secretariat employees, got to know about the attack through wireless messages, and also decided to move with their respective escort parties. Other senior officers of the city also moved towards the site.

4. The sentries were now feeling the pressure. They had lost one of their colleagues and had not even attended to the dead constable when the officers and their escort parties started moving in. Absence of electricity was making things even more difficult. They had one search light which could run only for an hour. The SSP directed the DySP (DAR) (District Armed Reserve) to send some more search lights to the police colony, anticipating a long drawn operation. It was not certain at this stage as to where the 'fidayeen'

attackers were hiding. The firing had stopped for the moment.

5. The SSP took stock of the situation. He immediately formed a squad of twenty policemen to take charge of the outer cordon of the colony to prevent escape of the terrorists by scaling the boundary wall. There were ten building blocks inside the colony. No civilian was seen moving outside and all the family members had gone inside their houses. The guard commander informed the SSP that the attackers were dressed up as policemen. The SSP took his escort party and one column of the SOG and cleared the first building block by searching each flat one by one. All the police families were safe inside the first block. The area behind the first block was made a makeshift assembling area for any police party or officer who tried to move in. Two bullet-proof bunkers were called in to act as a shield for the officers assembling at this place. It was important that the police parties were properly briefed about the situation and duties assigned to each in a manner so that there was least confusion and clarity of action. One bullet proof Gypsy vehicle manned by the SP (Operations) was tasked with the duty of patrolling the roads inside the colony so that the movement of the terrorists inside the colony was restricted. Headlights of the police Gypsy also lighted up the area and movement of personnel could be monitored.

6. By 9 PM all officers had arrived on the spot. The SSP took a short briefing session about the work done till that time and about the duties to be performed by each team. While the SP (Operations) was tasked to be on mobile duty in bullet-proof vehicles, three teams were formed to search and secure rest of the nine building blocks. Among the team leaders were the SDPO (CS), DySP (Operations)

and the SP (North). The teams were instructed to be in bullet proof jackets and helmets and to follow the house intervention drills in case the houses were locked from inside or outside. In a situation where the owner of the house was present inside, his help was to be sought to search the house. One team under the command of one DySP was assigned the duty of evacuation of the injured persons and of shifting the dead bodies to the mortuary. Bullet proof bunkers were utilized for this purpose. One team was stationed at the nearby hospital to liaise with the doctors and to keep them ready for handling any emergency.

7. A team of policemen was stationed by the DySP (DAR) at the hospital to arrange for the blood of any type required at the hospital. The local SHO was tasked with the duty of starting the investigation process and to ensure that no object of any evidentiary value was destroyed, lost, or tampered. A fully armed team was assigned with the SHO to ensure his safety and the safety of the forensic team accompanying him. A doctor from the police hospital was stationed in the first block to take care of any immediate requirement of first aid. One DySP was asked to arrange food for the officers and men involved in the operation. By now the media had got the news about the 'fidayeen' attack at the police colony, and a long queue of media vans and media personnel had gathered outside the boundary wall with their cameras focused towards the colony. Some of them even climbed up the nearby trees to get a glimpse of what was going on inside. The SSP assigned the task of handling the media personnel to an experienced police officer, the Additional SP (Headquarters). He ensured that the media personnel were briefed after every one hour and at the same time persuaded not to enter in the premises. Those trying to climb up the trees were explained that they

could be the victims of any stray bullet from inside. They followed the instructions and came down.

8. The police team formed to search the building blocks started their job carefully, clearing and declaring each flat free from terrorists. After clearing each block, two sentries in buddy pairs were kept at the entrance of the block to ensure that the attackers did not enter that block. Each flat owner was asked individually about his safety. Even if the owner certified that there were no terrorists inside, the rooms were searched and cleared to ensure that no hostage like situation was there inside the flats. Announcements were also made asking the hiding terrorists to surrender but there was no response from their side. While a team was searching the building block number seven, a burst of bullets was fired from the back side of the building which was completely dark. Electricity supply had resumed by that time and the terrorists hiding there could see the search parties, searching the flats one by one. Immediately after hearing the sound of fire, the lights of that building block were switched off so that the terrorists could not have a clear aim at the search party. The search parties barely managed to escape in the firing by the terrorists, however they continued the search. One team was assigned to fire single shots in the general direction from which the terrorists had fired in order to give cover fire to the search parties.

9. It was not sure whether the terrorists were present only behind block 7 or they were present in some other blocks also. The SSP asked all the teams on the wireless set to continue with their assigned search duties and not to leave their respective areas of search. He himself took a team of eight policemen and went to the first floor of block number 7 which had been cleared by then. He instructed

one of his men to focus his searchlight towards the back side without sticking out any of his body part in the line of fire. While the searchlight was focused on the back side, the SSP himself tried to spot the hiding terrorist from another window which was completely in the dark. Soon, the terrorist hiding in the back fired a burst of bullets at the person holding the searchlight, thereby breaking the searchlight. By this time, the SSP had spotted the terrorists hiding behind a tree.

10. Two teams of two policemen each were now stationed outside the block 7 in a manner that the terrorists could not leave the back side of block 7. Headlights of the police vehicles were used to illuminate both the escape routes of terrorists. While the SSP was in the process of organizing his men, the hiding terrorists lobbed a hand grenade towards the side where the IG, DIG and their escort parties were present. Five policemen sustained splinter injuries in this attack. The DIG also sustained splinter injuries on his leg and near his left eye. All the officers and men hurried back to safety. There was now a new task at hand, to evacuate the DIG and the other injured policemen to the nearby hospital. The same DySP who was earlier assigned the task to shift the injured persons was assigned this job. The SSP himself ensured that in this commotion focus on the hiding terrorists was not lost. The four men tasked to prevent escape of the terrorists from the back side of block 7 stuck to their duties.

11. Injury to a senior officer was a setback for the police party. The SSP had to hold his men together so that the morale of the police force was maintained. He gave a pep talk to his commanders on the wireless set and urged them to strike back at the terrorists with double vigour. He took a stalk of the search parties who were tasked with clearing

all the building blocks. The commanders reported about the status of searches in their respective areas. The SSP asked each one to stay in their assigned areas and not to leave their positions. Guards had now been put in front of all the buildings to ensure that no terrorist could enter the blocks and take any family hostage. It was now clear that there were only two terrorists and they were holed up on the back side of block 7 behind a tree. The task was now simpler. It was now 1 AM at night. The SSP decided to wait for the first light to take on the terrorists. Cordon of the area was strengthened and bullet-proof vehicles were stationed at vantage points. The SSP tasked each one of their commanders to keep making rounds of their respective areas to ensure that the policemen were alert. At the same time food packets were prepared and distributed among the police personnel who were on duty for the night. Police personnel deployed in the close vicinity of the place where the terrorists were hiding were replaced by fresh police personnel after every two hours and the previous ones were given food at the ear-marked place.

12. At around 5.30 AM, the hiding terrorists made a last attempt to run through the cordon of the police by firing indiscriminately. An alert police constable on the top of the bullet-proof bunker retaliated and both the terrorists got killed in the exchange of fire.

13. A wireless message was immediately flashed regarding culmination of the operation. The SSP took time out to brief the media personnel who had waited the whole night for some news about the operation. The police officers, who had not been allowed to enter the premises due to the progress of the operation, were allowed to rejoin with their families.

14. A need was felt to increase the strength of the police guard at the police housing colony which was immediately done. A standard SOP was formed by the SSP for the guard personnel on duty to ensure that the mistakes committed by them were not repeated by them or by the guards at other VIP locations or at sensitive installations.

Analysis

1. A clearance given by the house owner need not always mean that the terrorists are not hiding in the house. There can be a situation where the terrorists may take one of the members of the house as a hostage and force the house owner to give a clear signal to the search party.
2. In case searchlights are used for watching movements of terrorist in a dark area, the person using the searchlight should take adequate care as the hiding terrorists can see his movements and fire at him.
3. In any situation where police officers from different areas converge for an operation, there is a great need for a proper briefing and division of duties. In this case the SSP ensured that the parties were briefed and assigned specific duties in order to avoid confusion.
4. There should always be an experienced officer to deal with the media in such a sensitive situation. Media persons should not be allowed to move very close to the operational area in any case.
5. In case of an operation at night if the terrorists are surrounded, it is always advisable to wait for the first light to finish off the operation. Night operations can only be continued in case arrangements can be made to continuously light up the area of operation.

7. Operation in a Small Town

1. It was a cold afternoon in the month of February. At about 1430 hours the Additional Superintendent of Police (Addl SP) had just come back to his office from his house after taking lunch when a 'source' came to his office and claimed that he had information about presence of the most wanted terrorist commander of the sub-division in a house in the town. This house, according to the 'source', was in mohalla 'M', located at a distance of about 1 km from the police complex within which the police station, office of the Sub-Divisional Police Officer and the office of the Addl SP were located.
2. Initially to the Addl SP this information seemed improbable, for, a known terrorist could not have dared to remain in the town during day time, and that too at a place so close to the police establishment. The 'source' however, was very confident and wanted the operation to be conducted very fast as the terrorist, according to his information, was to leave this house soon after the sunset. The 'source' also demanded a very heavy amount for giving the information. He also put a condition that if the operation would not result in killing/arrest of the terrorist, and if the terrorist escaped during the operation but his presence in the house was confirmed, then also the Addl SP would have to pay him the same amount of money for giving information about the terrorist, as would be given to him in case of arrest/killing of the terrorist. The 'source' also maintained that in case his demands were not accepted by the Addl SP then he would prefer sharing the information with some other security forces stationed in the town.
3. During the bargaining over the reward money to be given to him, the 'source' remained totally adamant about his

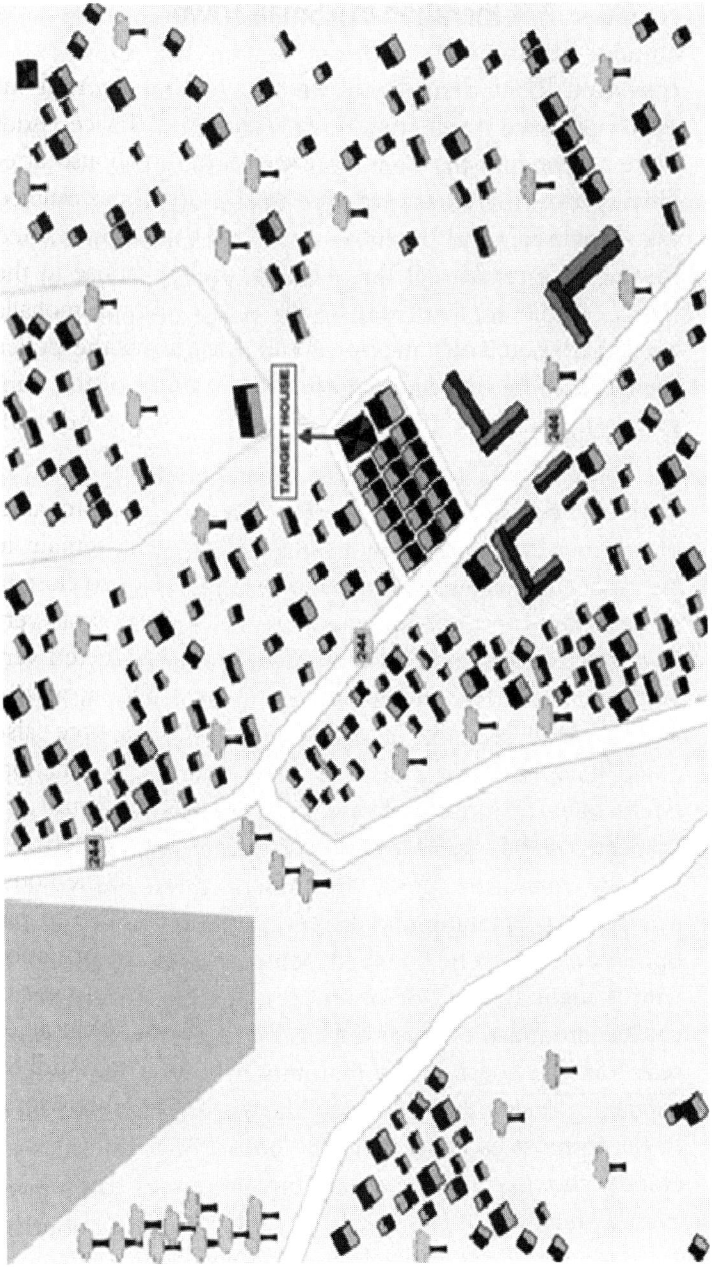

Operation in a Small Town.

conditions for sharing the information. After about half-an-hour of discussion with the 'source' the Addl SP got convinced about credibility of the 'source' and accepted his demands. Since it was winters, only about three hours were there to conduct the operation for arrest of the terrorist. Having decided to launch the operation, the Addl SP asked the SHO and In-charge of Special Operation Group to quickly assemble all the available police personnel for the operation. Total strength of the police personnel which could be immediately mustered within such a short notice came out to be only about forty.

4. It was going to be a very tricky operation. First, because the house in which the terrorist was reportedly hiding was in thickly populated area, thereby increasing the chances of collateral damages. Any mistake resulting in killing of an innocent civilian would have resulted in massive law and problems in the communally sensitive town. Secondly, in this operation, in case of a possible exchange of firing with the terrorist, which was quite probable, no area weapon, like grenade launcher or even a machine gun could have been used because use of such area weapon could have resulted in heavy collateral damages as the suspected house was located in a thickly populated area. Thirdly, very little time, only about three hours, was available for planning and executing the operation as the operation had to be finished before sunset. In the cold winter night it was not practically possible to keep the cordon around the house during the night time and start search of the house in the morning. In case of the cordon continuing during the night time, there was a high possibility of the terrorist escaping from the house. Also, the sky was cloudy and there were strong indications of rainfall or even a snowfall.

5. After having struck the deal with the 'source' the Addl SP asked the 'source' to accompany him in a civil vehicle and show the house. The 'source' readily agreed and while sitting along with the Addl SP in a slowly moving civil vehicle, he showed the double storied 'target house' to the Addl SP. This house had two approaches—one through a lane, about 200 metres long, leading to the house from the market area on the main road of the town, and another from the backside, through the same lane from the main Road passing by the side of the target house and opening on a narrow road in the backside of the house, about 30 metres from the target house. After having seen the target house the Addl SP planned to approach the target house using two police parties, from both the sides—from main road side as well as from the narrow road on the backside of the 'target house'. It appeared likely that in the event of seeing a police party from the back side, the terrorist would try to escape through the lane leading to the main road as from this side he would get opportunity to escape in many directions, taking advantage of the movement of large number of people/ vehicle on the main road. The Addl SP therefore planned to block this lane for stopping the terrorist in case he escaped through this route, and simultaneously send the search party to approach the target house from the back side.
6. Having decided the operational planning, the Addl SP first went to the Camp of the Special Operation Group (SOG) and without telling the exact details of the operation, properly briefed the police personnel, especially about strict control of firing in case of a possible exchange of firing with the terrorist as the area of operation was thickly populated. Thereafter, in a civil vehicle, he took

the Sub-Inspector in-charge of the SOG along with him, showed him the target house and asked him to put stops in the lane leading to the 'target house' from the main road. The Sub-Inspector was specifically asked to deploy police personnel in pairs on the entry of all the houses in this lane in order to prevent entry of the escaping terrorist in any of the houses located along the lane, making the operation further complicated. The Sub-Inspector was thereafter dropped in the SOG Camp and asked to move on foot along with his party from the Camp on the main road and from the main road towards the target lane, as if they were on a routine patrolling on the main road.

7. Thereafter, the Addl SP reached the Police Station and without telling the exact location of the 'target house' briefed the police personnel that they had to go for a search operation for arrest of a terrorist hiding in a house. This police party was divided in two groups—one party was briefed to lay a cordon around the 'target house' on the direction of the Addl SP when the party would reach close to the 'target house', while the other party, the search party planned to be led by the Station House Officer of the police station, was briefed to conduct search of the target house after getting a signal from the Addl SP when the cordon was completely laid down around the 'target house'. All the police personnel were put in a police station vehicle 'troop carrier' and the vehicle was asked to follow the vehicle of the Addl SP. The timing was planned in such a manner that before the cordon and the search party accompanying the Addl SP would reach the 'target house' from the road on the backside of the 'target house', the other police party comprising of the SOG personnel by that time would have put stops in the lane passing through the 'target house' and leading to the main road.

8. The Police personnel of the SOG reached the lane opening on the main road and the Sub-Inspector in-charge informed the Addl SP that they were about to put stops in the lane as directed. At this point the Addl SP along with the police party started from the police station and within 5/6 minutes reached the 'target house' where the Addl SP stopped his vehicle and showed the target house to the accompanying police personnel. The cordon party quickly laid the cordon around the 'target house'. In-charge SOG also intimated over the wireless set that stops had been laid in the lane leading to the main road. It was now the time to start search of the house. Before starting the search, the Addl SP located owner of the house and asked him to tell his family members to vacate the house. The house owner, however, flatly denied presence of any terrorist in his house and also agreed to help the police in conducting search of the house which had a total of about 7/8 rooms on the ground and the first floor. While the Addl SP remained on the ground floor of the house, the search party led by the Station House Officer started searching all the rooms of the house along with the house owner. After sometime the Station House Officer from the first floor of the house intimated the Addl SP that he had searched all the rooms but no body was found.
9. By this time only about half-an-hour was left before the sunset. Visibility was decreasing, also because the sky was getting overcast with clouds, with indications of rains or snowfall. On 'NTR' (Nothing to Report) by the SHO, the Addl SP thought of calling off the operation. But before deciding to do so he again asked the SHO whether he had checked all the rooms on the first floor of the house as the 'source' who had given information to the Addl SP about presence in the house was sounding

very confident. After about five minutes the SHO intimated the Addl SP that he had properly checked all the rooms and nothing was found but there was one room on the first floor which was locked and the house owner had told the SHO that this room was being used as a store room.

10. This made the Addl SP suspicious. He asked the SHO to get the lock of the room opened by the house owner. The Addl SP also asked the SHO to take position around the locked room, and that no police person should be in front of the wooden door of the room. The house owner appeared a little hesitant in opening the lock of the door, saying he would have to look for the key of the lock. The SHO conveyed this to the Addl SP which made the Addl SP even more suspicious and he alerted all the police personnel to take proper cover. The SHO thereafter asked the house owner to quickly get the key of the lock; otherwise he would break the lock put on the door of the locked room.

11. The terrorist hiding inside this locked room was listening to the conversation. Sensing trouble he thought of escaping from the house and for this purpose he first threw a hand grenade from the window of the room on the cordon party. The grenade exploded on the other side of boundary wall of the house and no damage was caused to the police personnel. This however confirmed the presence of the terrorist. The Addl SP then quickly got all the civilians/residents of the house shifted to one of the rooms on the ground floor and also tactically repositioned the police personnel of the cordon party. The terrorist in the meantime, threw another hand grenade on the cordon party and jumped out on the ground from the window of the first floor. In the grenade blast a 12 year old boy, who

was working as a domestic help in the house sustained splinter injuries.

12. After jumping on to the ground, the terrorist, while indiscriminately firing on the police party started running towards the lane leading to the main road. The Addl SP directed two of the police personnel to shift the injured boy, the domestic help, to the hospital (where he died subsequently) and along with three police personnel chased the fleeing terrorist. The police personnel chasing the terrorist however did not open fire on the fleeing terrorist as the fleeing terrorist was not firing on them and also the chasing police party could not see any weapon with the terrorist. The terrorist was wearing a 'phiran' (a kind of long gown completely covering the body) and was carrying a pistol in his hand concealed inside the 'phiran'. After going to some distance in the lane leading to the main road, the fleeing terrorist however got trapped in the lane between the police party chasing him from the back and the police party under the command of Sub-Inspector in-charge of the SOG who had already put a stop in the lane. Finding the Sub-Inspector in the front, the terrorist took out his hand carrying the pistol from the 'phiran' and fired upon the Sub-Inspector leading the SOG party. In the firing by the terrorist the Sub-Inspector sustained bullet injury in his thigh and fell down. However, the Sub-Inspector and the other police personnel retaliated the firing. In the exchange of firing the trapped terrorist got killed. Subsequently during search of the place of incident as well as from the possession of the killed terrorist one pistol with one magazine and two rounds, two wireless sets, one hand grenade, etc were recovered. Soon after the operation was over, after about twenty minutes, it started snowing, and it snowed very heavily, throughout the night.

Analysis

1. Success of an operation depends to a great extent on the planning of the operation. A search operation for arrest of a terrorist hiding in a house should be very carefully planned. The police party going for the operation should be fully prepared to deal with the situation of a possible exchange of fire.
2. Time becomes a crucial factor in an operation sometimes. In this operation a delay of even one hour would have resulted in failure of the operation or casualties of the police personnel.
3. Leadership in the operation is very important. The officer leading the operation should focus on all the aspects during the operation. It is not very important for him to fire himself, but more important is to control firing by the police personnel under his command.
4. Maximum care should be taken during the house search and room intervention. For example, in this case, while the SHO was trying to get the locked room open, the terrorist hiding inside the room could have fired from inside on the police party through the closed wooden door when the police personnel were trying to open the lock, and this would have resulted in casualties of the police personnel.

8. Operation at a Village in the Hotbed of Militancy

1. This case study is about an incident which took place in a small village located in a highly terrorism affected area. This area, bordering another highly terrorism affected district, had a large concentration of terrorists. Majority of the inhabitants in the area supported the terrorists, primarily under pressure from the terrorists, and also due to influence of the separatist elements.

2. Operating in this area had always been difficult for the police/security forces because of many reasons. First, the terrain was hilly. The terrorists sitting on small hillocks could easily see an approaching police party and open fire on them. Secondly, there were lots of apple orchards in the area. Hilly terrain coupled with thick vegetation in the area due to apple orchards, made it practically very difficult for the police to operate in the area. In the event of a face-off with police/security force the terrorist could easily escape taking advantage of the terrain and the thick vegetation. To facilitate their escape the terrorists had even issued diktats to the owners of the orchards not to put barbed wire or any kind of fencing around their orchards. Thirdly, very few 'sources' could be developed in the area by the police because majority of the people residing in the area either supported the terrorists under the influence of the separatist elements or had fears of the terrorists. In the past the terrorists had killed a good number of civilians in the area on the suspicion of them being 'sources' of the police/security forces. Barely a few days before the operation the terrorists had killed a police constable in a very gruesome manner; his head was chopped off and kept in a public place while the torso was kept at some other place, and the police had to put in a lot of efforts in locating it. Fourthly, because of being in the area bordering two districts, the area received less attention by the police of both the districts. Coordination between police of the two districts also remained an issue.
3. It was the month of October. The winter had just started setting in. Leaves of the apple trees had started falling off, increasing the visibility through the orchards. It was expected that with the onset of winter and decreasing temperature, especially during the nights, the terrorists

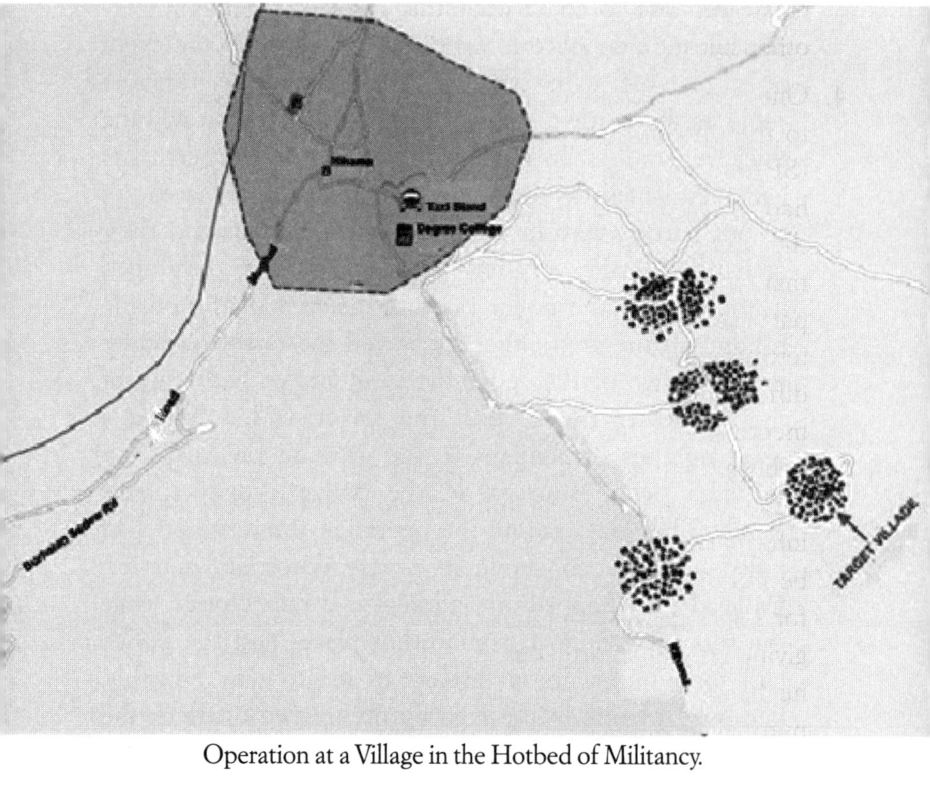

Operation at a Village in the Hotbed of Militancy.

would stay in some house during the night time. Experiences suggested that normally, soon after dark, a terrorist would enter in a house, spend the night in that house, and would leave the house before the day-break in the morning. There were also some chances that after entering into a house and having food there, the terrorists, in order to create deception, would leave that house and enter some other house to spend the night.

4. One evening, at about 11 PM in the night, a 'source' came to the official residence of the Superintendent of Police (SP) of the district and informed him that two terrorists had entered into the house of a particular civilian in the village late in the evening. The 'source' claimed that he had himself seen the terrorists entering inside the particular house and personally knew one of the two terrorists, who was a local of that area. Initially, it was very difficult for the SP to believe the 'source' as the SP was meeting him for the first time and it was difficult to believe that a person would take so much of risk to come out of the village and come to the SP in the night, informing him about presence of terrorists. It appeared to be more of a 'trap'. However, after talking to the 'source' for some time the SP could make out that the source was giving correct information as the 'source' mentioned that he had personal enmity against that terrorist who was putting pressure on his father to get his sister married to him. The 'source' also volunteered to accompany the police party which finally made the SP to believe that it was not going to be a 'trap'. The SP thereafter decided to launch a cordon and search operation in the village for arrest of the terrorists.

5. According to the plan, a team of Special Operation Group (SOG) of police in bullet proof bunkers, accompanied by

the 'source' who was also dressed up like a police official, reached the village at about 2 AM in the night. The vehicles were stopped about 2 km before the village and from there the policemen marched on foot. Stopping of the vehicles away from the target village was necessary as the sound of the vehicles could have alerted the terrorists. After reaching close to the village the SOG personnel first laid an outer cordon around the village, little away from the village, as going closer to the village could have given indication to the terrorists, mainly due to the barking of the dogs during any movement.

6. While the cordon party laid a tight cordon around the village sealing all the possible escape routes, the search party patiently waited for the dawn as even though the 'source' was willing to take the search part directly to the 'target house', search of the house in the night time could have resulted in damages to the police personnel, even by themselves. Also there was a possibility of the terrorists having shifted to some other house in the village, after they were spotted by the 'source' entering in the 'target house, in the evening hours.

7. Early in the morning when the search party was about to start search of the 'target house', the terrorists hiding in the house came out of the house, and tried to escape by firing upon the search party. However, upon effective retaliation by the search party both the terrorists entered inside a double-storied house of another villager. The search party thereafter quickly surrounded this house and took effective position around the house.

8. A tricky situation developed however, as the search party was told by the villagers that some civilians were also present in the house in which the terrorists had taken shelter. Before resorting to house intervention therefore,

the civilians trapped inside the house were to be evacuated first, as a possible exchange of firing between the terrorists and the search party could have resulted in civilians being caught in the cross firing. Upon being asked by the police party to surrender and let the trapped villagers come out, the terrorists refused to let the trapped villagers come out of the house and demanded safe passage, failing which, they threatened, that they would kill the civilians.

9. The matter was reported to the district SP soon after the occurrence following which the SP along with additional police force immediately rushed to the village. On the way the SP also requested the nearby security force Camp In-charge to accompany him to the village along with his force which the Camp In-charge readily agreed. Upon reaching the village an assessment of the situation was made. To begin with it was not very clear as to how many civilians were trapped inside the house. After the initial exchange of firing between the terrorists and the police party, most of the villagers had left their houses and the number and identity of the civilians who were trapped inside the house could not be clearly established. In order to persuade the terrorists the 'village headman' was called and was asked to request the terrorists on the loudspeaker of the village mosque to let the civilians come out of the house. However, despite repeated requests by the village headman, the terrorists did not let the trapped civilians come out of the house. A hostage kind of situation therefore developed which attracted attention of the print as well as electronic media and a large number of media persons assembled near the village. A rumour was also spread that the police personnel during the search operation had themselves sent the civilians inside the house, who were in turn taken as hostages by the terrorists, and that, the police had used the civilians as 'human shield' in the operation.

10. The SP was therefore under great pressure to first get the trapped civilians rescued without any harm. Due to peculiarity of the situation, the other security forces present on the spot also were very hesitant to take any step, fearing the blame being shifted on them in case of any mishap. The option of house intervention was totally ruled out, more so, because the terrorists were claiming that they were four in number and there were sixteen civilians inside the house whom they were threatening to kill if safe passage was not given to them. A lot of commotion also could be heard inside the house, civilians crying and pleading the theorists to let them go and the terrorists shouting at them, asking them to keep quite. Though the figure of sixteen appeared to be on the higher side, presuming that the terrorists were quoting exaggerated figure for a good bargain, it was assessed that the number of trapped civilians would be around five to six.

11. After the terrorists did not positively respond to the requests of the 'village headman' to let the civilians come out of the house, the SP somehow established contact with the terrorists on a radio set and tried to negotiate with the terrorists. By this time it was around 5 o'clock in the evening and with the help of the other security forces a tight cordon was laid around the house. Lighting arrangements were also made using the generator sets making the surroundings of the house well lit, so that the terrorists could not escape during the night time.

12. Another incident also happened late in the afternoon. In view of the importance of the operation a very senior officer of one of the security forces involved in the operation was coming to the spot. As his vehicle, escorted by 2 other vehicles, reached closed to the spot, about 3-4 km before the village, a powerful IED (Improvised Explosive Device)

blast was caused by the terrorists in which the officer had a very narrow escape. Later, in the evening, firing shots were also heard from the areas surrounding the village which led to the apprehension that the associates of the trapped terrorists might try to attack the police/security forces from behind. Also, lot of movement of the police/security forces vehicles was taking place on the road linking the village to the nearby sub-divisional town to bring food, arms/ammunition, additional forces, etc. Further, after the operation all the police and other security force personnel had to go back from the village following the same route. Hence, a strong ROP (Route Opening Party) was deployed on the road, linking the village to the nearby sub-divisional town.

13. Negotiation with the terrorists by the SP on the radio set continued till about 1 AM in the night. The SP mainly tried to impress upon the terrorists not to involve civilians in conflicts with the police/security forces as the so-called 'jehad' by the terrorists was ostensibly for the people itself. Additional District Magistrate also tried to persuade the terrorists to leave the civilians taken as hostages. In between the discussions with the terrorist and the SP, a senior officer of a security force also talked to the terrorists sounding very tough. This however proved to be counter-productive, the terrorists refusing to talk any more. However after repeated persuasion by the SP for quite some time the terrorists again agreed to resume the negotiations. The SP finally offered to the terrorists that they would be given safe passage next morning in front of local/national print and electronic media, provided the civilians were set free by the terrorists without causing any harm to them. This proposal appealed to the terrorists and they replied that they would consider this proposal in the morning and would get back to the SP.

14. There was still no hope. The pressure was mounting on the police but there seemed to be no proper way by which the civilians could be safely rescued. Talking with the terrorists however gave a fairly good idea that the terrorists were not more than three, out of whom at least one was a local terrorist as he was talking in the local 'Kashmiri' language and was relatively soft in the negotiations, while at least one terrorist was a non-local as he did not know the local language and used to intervene in the discussion, speaking in Urdu. Talking with the terrorists also gave a fair indication that the trapped civilians were not more than five to six, and definitely not 15/16 which the terrorists were claiming.
15. At about 5 AM, just before the day-break, in-charge of escort party of the SP, a Head Constable, came to the SP and suggested the SP to have a look of the house along with him. After going very close to the house he pointed to a window of the house which was half closed. The Head Constable suggested firing of tear gas shells inside the house. He also suggested putting some mattresses on the ground close to the window so that a person could jump over it from the double-storeyed house, without being harmed.
16. The idea given by the Head Constable appealed to the SP. Mattresses were quickly arranged from the nearby houses and three 'tear gas guns' along with short rage tear gas shells, which were normally kept in the escort vehicles of the SP were quickly brought near the house. Thereafter in quick succession, tear-gas shells were fired inside the first floor of the house through the window. Following this, after about two to three minutes, two of the civilians taken as hostages, opened one of windows to take fresh air. Both of them were exhorted by the police party to jump out on the ground, on the mattresses, which they did and were

brought to a safer place by the police party. Subsequently, four more civilians jumped out on the ground in the similar manner and were brought to a safer place. All the six civilians were then brought to a house nearby, on the first floor of which the SP and senior officers of the other security forces had temporarily made a joint command room. Questioning of these six rescued civilians revealed that only six civilians were taken as hostages and no more civilian was left inside the house. The rescued civilians also revealed that there were only two terrorists inside the house. All the rescued civilians, who were in great shock and trauma, were comforted and made to sit on the ground floor of the house.

17. Later, the two terrorists hiding inside the house also tried to escape by firing upon the police party but got killed in the ensuing exchange of fire with the police and the accompanying security forces. The rescued civilians however, had another providential escape from death; this time from the security forces itself. After being rescued they were made to sit on the ground floor of a house, on the first floor of which senior officers of all the security forces were camping. While the rescued civilians were taking tea, the terrorists in order to escape, suddenly fired indiscriminately from the house in which they were hiding. A wireless operator of a very senior officer of one of the security forces, who was with the officer on the first floor alongside of the officer, was carrying an AK rifle, in loaded position, with his finger on the trigger. When the terrorists suddenly fired indiscriminately, the wireless operator, in sudden panic, pressed the trigger resulting in a burst of fire coming out of his rifle which was pointed downwards. The bullets, which came out of his rifle, pierced through the wooden floor of the first floor of the house and hit the ground floor, very narrowly missing one of the rescued civilians.

Analysis

1. In a hostage like situation, as was there in this case, it is very important to keep the terrorists engaged in order to buy time. For this, the most important thing is to somehow establish contact with the terrorists. While talking to them, the negotiator should sound sympathetic to the terrorists, giving them the feeling that there are chances of them getting a safe passage.
2. In case of an operation in which more than one security forces are involved, a temporary joint-command room should be established from where they can coordinate the operation jointly and can also discuss the situation and take decisions accordingly.
3. Proper briefing of the police party is very important, especially about carrying of the arms. The police personnel going for an operation need to keep their arms in loaded position but 'safety catch' should be on, and in any case finger should not be on the trigger. Otherwise, a policeman may react in panic, causing avoidable damages to his own colleagues or to any other person, as could have happened in this case.
4. When an operation takes place in a remote area which is highly terrorism affected, the route leading to the place of incident should also be properly secured. Securing of the route leading to the place of operation becomes more important in case the operation is likely to continue for a long time because under this situation, sometimes additional forces would be required to be brought to the operation site. Also, food and other logistics would also have to be brought to the operation site. Besides senior officers also often come to the site of the operation for whom there should be proper security arrangements.

5. In an operation like the one discussed above, the police personnel who are deployed in the outer most cordon feel more relaxed as they are least likely to face firing from the terrorists. However, they need to be properly briefed before start of the operation and also kept in alert position. This is required for two reasons; one, that they should be able to take on a terrorist who would try to break out of the inner cordon while escaping; and secondly, there can be a possibility that the associates of the trapped terrorist, in order to divert attention of the inner cordon/search party and create confusion, may attack the police personnel deployed in the outer cordon and inflict damage on them if they are not properly alert.
6. In an operation, which drags on for a longer time, the officer leading the police party should be very careful at the time of withdrawal from the place of operation. This is because the terrorists operating in the area also become fully aware about position of the police party and they also become aware that after end of the operation, the police party would be withdrawing from predictable routes. Hence the route through which the police party is to be withdrawn after the operation, should be secured before starting withdrawal of the operation. The party securing the route should also tactfully withdraw after all the police personnel deployed in the operation are withdrawn.

9. Operation in an Urban Area

1. This case study is related to an operation which took place in a thickly populated locality in the heart of a town which always had a large support base of the separatist elements. It was last day of the year. There was a general mood of celebration in the town, particularly because 'Eid' was to

be celebrated the next day. There had been lot of activities in the town for the last three-four days in view of the 'Eid' celebrations. Lots of people were coming to the town from the nearby villages for purchasing gifts, etc. Since it was December, there was early sun set, and being the last day before the 'Eid', shopping activities in the town were also coming to a halt by the evening.

2. In the evening, by about 5 PM when the darkness had just started setting in, Additional Superintendent of Police (Addl SP) received information about movement of a notorious terrorist commander. The terrorist was reported to be moving with two of his associates in a thickly populated locality, located in the town. This 'Mohalla' was located by the side of the river, inhabited mostly by poor and illiterate people belonging to 'boatman' community. Houses in this locality were in very close vicinity; most of the houses did not even have a separation or a 'boundary wall' in between two houses.

3. Operating in this area had always been risky. Even a routine patrol of police was seldom sent in this area because of fears of possible attacks by the terrorists hiding in houses, who, after an attack on the police/security forces, could easily escape through the narrow lanes and by-lanes which were there in the area. In the past there had been numerous grenade attacks on the patrolling party of the police/security forces in this locality. Retaliation by the police/security forces had always been very limited due to fears of civilian casualties. The area was also being used as a good hideout by the terrorists as after committing a terrorist attack, the terrorists could easily conceal their weapon somewhere and cross over to the other side of the river Jhelum using a boat.

4. Given the sensitivity of the area and criticality of the situation, the next day being the day of 'Eid celebrations' besides being

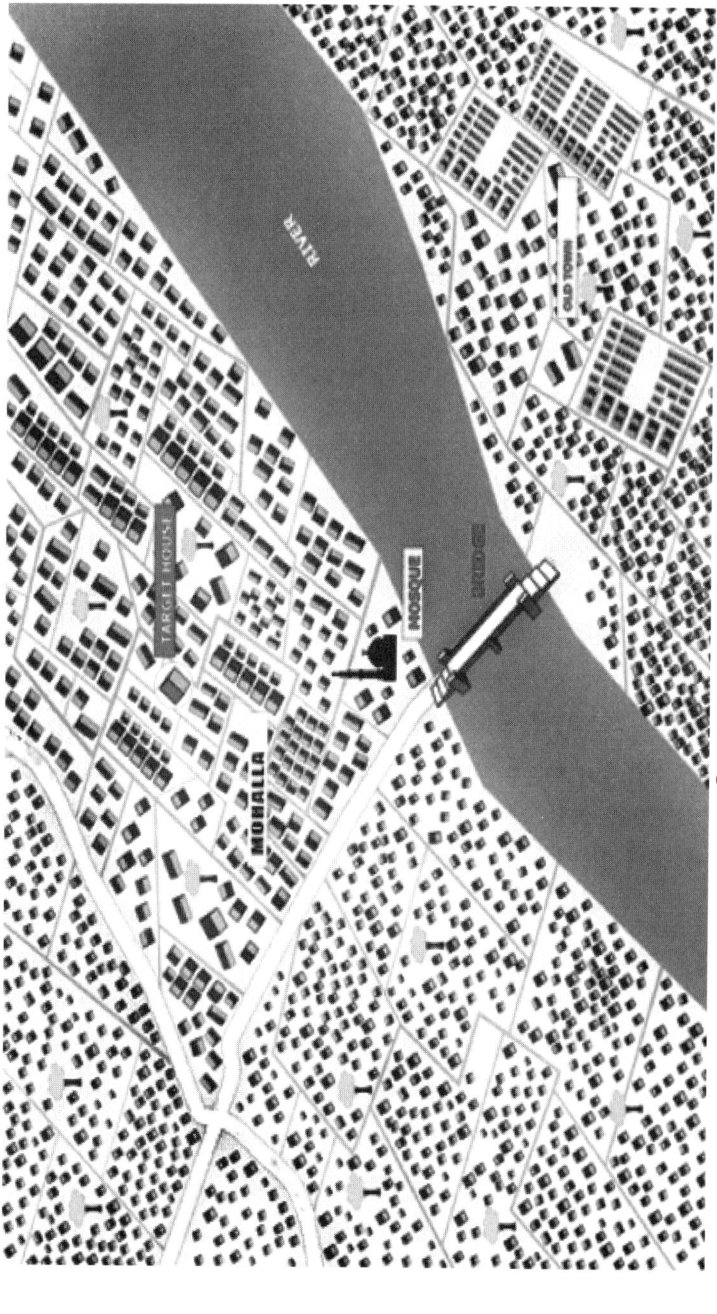

Operation in an Urban Area.

the 'New Year day', it was a difficult decision to launch an operation in the area. Any collateral damage could have resulted in massive protests the next day as large congregation of people was otherwise also expected for the 'Eid prayers' in the town, especially in the Jamia Masjid (the main masjid of the town), which was in the same locality in which movement of the three terrorists was reported. Further, operating in this highly terrorists affected area of the town after darkness would otherwise have been very risky for the police. Normally, tactics always suggested not to go for any operation in the evening after dark.

5. The Addl SP discussed the matter with the Senior Superintendent of Police (SSP) of the district. It was after a very long time that some credible information was received about this particular terrorist commander who was a local of the town and wielded considerable influence in the people. He was a terror as he used to act with impunity, killing a suspected informer of police/security forces in a barbaric manner. Just a couple of months ago, he had killed a doctor on the suspicion of him being an informer, by cutting his neck with a blade. After the killing, his head was kept by the terrorists in the main square of the town while his torso was kept in an apple orchard close to the town. A video film of the killing was also made which was circulated through mobile phones. Also, the car belonging to the killed 'informer' was burnt by the terrorists in front of the police station, late in the evening, after the darkness had just started setting in.

6. The option before the police was either to launch operation in the evening immediately taking the risk or to wait till late in the night and conduct search operation early in the morning, as used to be the standard operating procedure

for conducting operations. The second option, however, did not appear feasible in view of the 'Eid celebrations' the next day. Thus, the only two alternatives were to either abandon the operation or take the risk and start operation immediately, in the evening itself.

7. However, since very credible information about the terrorist commander was received by the police after a very long time, and also since according to the input the three terrorists, including the terrorist commander, were seen moving without weapons, it was decided to take the risk and launch the operation in the area for their arrest. Accordingly, the police party, under the command of the Addl SP and assisted by the security forces moved into the locality at about 7 PM in the evening. All the police/ security force personnel were properly briefed about being extra cautious in using their firearms in view of sensitivity of the operation.

8. The police, assisted by the security forces, conducted search operation in the locality for about one hour but they could not get any trace of the terrorists. Police personnel were also not very strict during the searches and were rather defensive during the operation in view of the peculiarity of the situation. At about 8 PM, the police and the security forces started withdrawing from the area. However, at about 8.15 PM the SSP got a technical input suggesting that the terrorists were trapped somewhere in the locality following which the operation was quickly re-launched and the SSP also rushed to the town.

9. In between, while the police and the other security force personnel were conducting searches in the locality, the terrorists hiding in a house, apprehending that they have been trapped, fired upon the police personnel. This confirmed the presence of the terrorists and the Addl SP

quickly laid a proper cordon around the target house. The SSP also reached the spot. Despite knowing the presence of the terrorist in a particular house the operation still was a difficult one. Under normal circumstances police could have waited till morning, and gone for house intervention on the first-light. In this case, in view of the 'Eid' festival on the next day, time available with the police was only up to the morning. But 'house intervention' during the night time could have been suicidal. Also, the house in which the terrorists were hiding, was an old, abandoned house, mostly made up of woods, and there were great chances of it catching fire which would, in turn, have also spread to the other houses in the vicinity, as the houses in that locality were very close to each other. Chances of the fire spreading to the other houses were more, also because most of people used to keep fire woods stored in the attic portion of their houses during the winter season.

10. Controlling the fire therefore became the most important thing at this stage of operation and quickly three 'fire brigades' were arranged at the place. A 'JCB' machine was also brought to the side to clear the debris in case the fire broke out. While all the alternatives to tackle the terrorists were being discussed, the terrorists sudden fired a heavy burst of firing on the police party and tried to escape but due to quick retaliatory firing by the police/security force personnel they went back inside the house. In the heavy exchange of firing, one side of the house in which the terrorists were hiding, caught fire. The fire-brigade personnel were put into service but they could not effectively control the fire because the terrorists were intermittently firing from the house and the fire-brigade personnel were also exposed to the risk of getting bullet injury. The strategy therefore was slightly modified and the fire brigade personnel were asked to continuously spray water on the houses

adjoining this target house in order to save them from being burnt. This required lot of water for which the fire brigade machines were innovatively connected, directly with the river Jhelum.

11. Another serious problem however cropped up. The news spread very quickly in the locality that the terrorist commander, who was a local, was trapped in the house, and that an exchange of fire was going on in the locality between the terrorists and the police/security forces. Following this, a large crowd, especially of young men/boys assembled around the operation site and while shouting religious slogans, started pelting stones on the police personnel who were in the outer most cordon. Police therefore had a very tough time tackling the mob throwing stones on the police personnel, primarily because it was night time and no previous planning was done to deal with this kind of situation. During the process, by about midnight, the house in which the terrorists were hiding totally got engulfed in fire but despite repeatedly being asked to come out and surrender, the terrorists did not attempt to come out of the house again, possibly realizing that they have been surrounded by the police/security force personnel from all the sides. Firing from the burning house after sometime however stopped giving indication that the terrorists had possibly died due to the fire. The fire brigade personnel thereafter put of the fire and with the help of the 'JCB' machine the debris was cleared from which charred dead bodies of the three terrorists were recovered besides arms and ammunition. The entire police/security force personnel were withdrawn by about 5 AM, before the first light. From a house close to the target house, a very big size IED (Improvised Explosive Device) was recovered which was brought by the explosive experts to the river side and blasted off at the break of the dawn, with a loud sound.

The New Year had begun on a positive note. Death of the terrorist led to a great decline in terrorist incidents in the town in the times to come.

Analysis

1. While operating in a sensitive area, where the terrorist/ insurgents have good support base, before launching an operation the police should also have a component to deal with law and order problems as happened in this case.
2. Before planning an operation on a sensitive occasion, a proper risk/benefit analysis should be done. A terrorist may be arrested later also, but possible collateral damages during the course of an operation on a sensitive occasion may not be worth taking the risk. Therefore, it should be carefully weighed whether to go for an operation on a day of important religious celebrations or not.
3. Before going for operations, advance planning and arrangements should be done to deal with situations such as a house catching fire during the operation. Fire-brigades should be brought to the spot immediately after launching the operation instead of asking for it when the fire has already started.

CHAPTER 2

Use of Force: Legal Perspectives

Homicide

During a police operation, when faced with armed offenders, use of force by the police by means of firearms may result in killing of the offender. Killing of the offender in police action is essentially a homicide as it involves killing of a (living) human being by a (living) human being. However, every homicide is not punishable in law. Section 6 of the Indian Penal Code (IPC) provides that throughout the Code every definition of an offence, every penal provision and every illustration of every such definition or penal provision, shall be understood subject to the exceptions contained in the chapter entitled 'General Exceptions' which provide complete exemption from criminal liability in situations envisaged therein even if the act of the offender falls in the definition of an offence under IPC. Thus, causing of death of the offender in exercise of Right of Private Defence within the limitations of this right as envisaged in the Chapter IV of IPC makes homicide lawful. Other defences envisaged in Chapter IV of IPC are acts done in pursuance of a lawful authority, or by reason of mistake of fact in good faith, or death caused by accident or misfortune or while doing an act in good faith and with no criminal intention for the benefit of the very person killed, makes homicide lawful. In other cases homicide caused with guilty mind becomes punishable under law as will be explained below.[1]

Homicide becomes unlawful in the following situations:

I. When it amounts to either culpable homicide amounting to murder under section 300 punishable under section 302 IPC or culpable homicide not amounting to murder punishable under section 304 Part-I or Part-II IPC, as the case may be. These offences result in the following situations:

    (a) In the scheme of IPC, culpable homicide is the genus and 'murder', its specie. All murders are culpable homicide but not *vice versa*. Culpable homicide is defined in section 299 and Murder is defined in section 300 of the IPC. Speaking generally culpable homicide 'sans' 'special characteristic of murder' is 'culpable homicide not amounting to murder'.

    (b) For the purposes of awarding punishment, proportionate to the gravity of the generic offence, IPC practically recognises three degree of culpable homicide. The first is what may be called, 'culpable homicide of the first degree'. This is the severest form of culpable homicide which is defined in section 300 as 'murder'. The second may be termed as 'culpable homicide of the second degree'. This is punishable under the first part of section 304 as 'culpable homicide not amounting to murder.' Then there is 'culpable homicide of the third degree'. This is the lowest type of culpable homicide and the punishment provided for it is also the lowest

1. The discussion hereunder is based on the two chapters authored by Prof BT Kaul published in Annual Survey of Indian Law, Volumes XXXVIII (2002) and XXXIX (2003) titled 'Criminal Law' (ASIL Vol XXXVIII Criminal Law 181 at 183 to 190 and ASIL Vol XXXIX Criminal Law 141 at 150 to 152).

> among the punishments provided for the three grades of culpable homicide. Culpable homicide of this degree is punishable under second part of section 304 IPC again as 'culpable homicide not amounting to murder'. The distinction between culpable homicide and murder is important keeping in view the punishment that eventually will be attracted is death or life imprisonment in case of 'murder' under section 302 IPC and lesser punishment in case of 'culpable homicide not amounting to murder' under first part of 304, with further lesser punishment in cases falling under second part of 304. Therefore, there is always an attempt on the part of the defence to at least persuade the court to hold that the accused is guilty of only culpable homicide not amounting to murder.

The proper way to bring out academic distinction between culpable homicide and murder is to examine whether the case at hand is covered by one of the three clauses of section 299 and if the answer is in affirmative, the act of the accused is culpable homicide. Thereafter, the next step is to see whether or not the case at hand also falls in one of the four clauses of section 300 so that the actual criminality of the accused is determined.

In the scheme of IPC the three clauses of section 299 are alternate clauses and each clause has a comparable clause in section 300 with distinction in the language used therein. Clause (a) of section 299 is comparable with clause (1) of section 300, clause (b) of section 299 with clauses (2) and (3) of section 300 and clause (c) of section 299 with clause (4) of section 300 IPC. It is important in each case to ascertain with clarity as to which of the three clauses of section 299 is attracted in a given case so that a further enquiry can be made in respect of corresponding comparable clause in section 300.

The language used in clause (a) of section 299 is identically similar to clause (1) of section 300. A case which falls in clause (a) of section 299 automatically falls in clause (1) of section 300 as well and, therefore, every case of culpable homicide falling in clause (a) of section 299 is a case of murder except in cases where the defence is able to bring the case at hand under one of the exceptions to section 300 which are in the form of partial defences in which case the criminality of the offender is reduced from what would have been otherwise a case of murder to culpable homicide not amounting to murder punishable under section 304 part-I, IPC.

Culpable homicide as defined in section 299 amounts to 'murder' if the prosecution succeeds in proving that the act of the accused falls in corresponding comparable clause in section 300 and the defence fails to bring the case of the accused in any of the exceptions to section 300 attracting punishment under section 302, IPC.

Culpable homicide does not amount to murder where either the act of accused though covered by clauses (b) or (c) of section 299 is not covered in the comparable clauses of section 300 or though covered even under the comparable clause of section 300 but at the same time the defence succeeds in bringing the case of the accused under one of the exceptions of section 300, IPC. In both these situations the accused is liable to be punished for only culpable homicide not amounting to murder and the punishment to be met out to the accused will depend upon whether the case of the accused falls under part-I or part-II of section 304, IPC. Section 304 part-I provides punishment in respect of cases of culpable homicide not amounting to murder which fall under clauses (a) and (b) of section 299. Section 304 part-II provides punishment in respect of cases of culpable homicide not amounting to murder which do not fall under clauses (a) and (b) of section 299 but fall under clause (c) of section 299.

Clause (b) of section 299 postulates intention of the accused to cause bodily injury which is present on the body of the deceased which is subjective enquiry in respect of the intention of the offender. However, in practice, if the accused fails to prove that the injury caused was accidental or unintentional the presumption of fact is that he intended to cause it. The second part of clause (b) of section 299 that the injury so caused is *likely to cause death* is a purely objective enquiry. The word *'likely'* in clause (b) of section 299 conveys the sense of *probable* as distinguished from a mere *possibility*. What is possible is not probable and what is probable is something more than possible. When the chances of death are more than that of survival we say death is a probability. Where the chances of death and survival are equally possible we can say that death is a possibility but not a probability. Therefore, the prosecution in section 299 clause (b) have to prove not only that accused intended to cause the bodily injury on the body of the deceased but has to prove that the injury so caused was likely to cause death and death has been caused. This part of the enquiry is purely an objective one and is independent of the intention of the accused. It is important to state that the two clauses of section 299(b) are disjunctive clauses. Having brought the case under clause (b) of section 299 the prosecution has further to prove that the case of the accused also falls either under clause 2 or clause 3 of section 300 so that the gravity of the charge is proved to be culpable homicide of first degree ie culpable homicide amounting to murder. The distinguishing feature of *mens rea* under clause (2) of section

300 is the *knowledge* possessed by the offender regarding the particular victim being in such a peculiar condition or state of health that the injury caused is likely to cause death of the victim, notwithstanding the fact that such harm is not sufficient to cause death in the ordinary course of nature of that person. This provision is specially provided to protect persons with physical infirmity or disease or disorder and, therefore, is intended to deter people from resorting to misadventures against such people. It is noteworthy that the 'intention to cause death' is not an essential requirement of clause (2). Only the intention of causing the bodily injury coupled with the offender's knowledge of the likelihood of such injury causing death of the victim is sufficient to bring the act of the accused within the ambit of this clause. This aspect of clause (2) is borne out by illustrations (b) appended to section 300.

Although clause (b) of section 299 does not postulate any such knowledge on the part of the offender explicitly but reading the said clause along with Explanation I to section 299 clearly brings to the fore that clause (b) of section 299 has to be read in two contexts. Firstly, we have to consider the act of the accused in relation to a person of normal health or a person of abnormal health but the abnormality aspect of the health is not within the knowledge of accused. In both these cases the act of the accused of causing bodily injury which is intentional bodily injury is to be objectively assessed in relation to its impact on a person of normal health. If death is likely (a probability) and the death of the victim has taken place, it is a case of culpable homicide. But if death of the accused was not probable and was only a possibility then it is not a case of culpable homicide even though death has taken place. Secondly, we have to consider the act of the accused in relation to a person of abnormal health and the accused having knowledge of the physical abnormality/infirmity of the victim. In such case if the bodily injury caused is intentional and the said bodily injury accelerates the death of the person due to bodily infirmity and the injury caused though not likely to cause the death of a person of normal health but is likely to cause the death of a person of abnormal health like the victim, the act of the accused is nonetheless culpable homicide. Here, the impact of the injury caused has to be assessed in relation to the persons of abnormal health and the likelihood of death to a person with such bodily infirmity, disease or disorder. If section 299(b) is not read in this context the purpose of providing Explanation I is defeated. Further, a case before it falls under sub-clause (2) of section 300 has to fall under section 299(b) and it is only when section 299(b) and Explanation I are so read that the intention of the legislature is truly reflected. The knowledge of the physical infirmity of the victim is implicit in section 299(b) when read along with Explanation I. This interpretation fully justifies comparison of section 299(b) with sub-section (2) of section 300.

Section 299 thus, has to be understood in two situations:

(i) cases where Explanation I to section 299 is attracted; and

(ii) cases where Explanation I to section 299 is not attracted.

Section 300 sub-clause (2) is comparable with situation (i) above and sub-clause (3) of section 300 is comparable with situation (ii) above.

Instances of cases falling under section 299 read with Explanation I and section 300 sub-clause (2) can be where the assailant causes death by fist blow intentionally given with the knowledge of the fact that the victim is suffering from an enlarged liver or enlarged spleen or disease of heart and such blow is likely to cause death of that particular person by the rupture of the liver or spleen or the failure of the heart, as the case may be. If the assailant had no such knowledge about the disease or special frailty of the victim or nor an intention to cause death the act of the accused would not be culpable homicide and, therefore, question of the same being murder would not arise. Every case of a person of abnormal health whose death is caused by an act of a human being must, before it falls under section 300 (2), first fall under section 299(b) IPC.

In clause (3) of section 300, instead of words 'likely to cause death' occurring in corresponding clause (b) of section 299, the words 'sufficient in the ordinary course of nature' have been used. The distinction is fine but real and if overlooked, may result in miscarriage of justice. The difference between clause (b) of section 299 and clause (3) of section 300 is one of degree of probability of death resulting from the intended bodily injury. To put it more broadly it is the degree of probability of death which determines whether a culpable homicide is of the gravest, medium or the lowest degree. The word 'likely' in clause (b) of section 299 conveys the sense of probable as distinguished from a mere possibility. The words 'bodily injury ... sufficient in the ordinary course of nature to cause death' means that the death will be most probable result of the injury having regard to the ordinary course of nature as distinguished from a mere sense of probability. To illustrate this distinction we may say that if the chances of death are more than 50% but less than 75% we can say death is not a mere possibility but is a probability. But if the chances of death are above 75% but not a certainty i.e. less than 100%

we say death is not mere probability but is most probable having regard to the ordinary course of nature.

For the cases to fall within clause (3) it is not necessary that the offender intended to cause death so long as the death ensues from the intentional bodily injury and the said bodily injury when objectively examined is not only 'likely' to cause death but is 'sufficient to cause death in the ordinary course of nature'. It is important again to stress here that the two parts of section (3) are disjunctive. The scope and meaning of the words used in clause (3) have been very lucidly explained by Vivian Bose J in Virsa Singh.[2] It was observed in that judgment that the prosecution must prove the following facts before a case can be brought under section 300 thirdly:

> "First, it must establish, quite objectively, that a bodily injury is present;
>
> Secondly, the nature of the injury must be proved; These are purely objective investigations.
>
> Thirdly, it must be proved that there was an intention to inflict that particular bodily injury, that is to say, that it was not accidental or unintentional, or that some other kind of injury was intended.
>
> Once these three elements are proved to be present, the enquiry proceeds further and,
>
> Fourthly, it must be proved that the injury of the type just described made up of the three elements set out above is sufficient to cause death in the ordinary course of nature. This part of the enquiry is purely objective and inferential and has nothing to do with the intention of the offender."

These tests have consistently been reiterated in all subsequent decisions having bearing upon section 300(3),

2. AIR 1958 SC 465.

IPC and have become *locus classicus* and which are now ingrained in our legal system and have become part of the rule of law.

Clause (c) of section 299 and clause (4) of section 300 neither require intention to kill nor intention to cause bodily injury as *mens rea* but both require knowledge of the probability of act causing death as necessary *mens rea*. Section 299(c) requires that the accused must have caused bodily injury with the knowledge that the act is likely to death. The *mens rea* required is not actual knowledge but the knowledge that can be attributable to a person of normal mind. If he does the act voluntarily he ought to know the likely consequence of his act. Illustrations (b) and (c) of section 299 fully illustrate this situation. A mother with her child in her arm jumps into the well and the mother survives but the child dies. Mother is guilty of culpable homicide as she ought to have known that jumping in the well with the child is likely to cause the death of the child even though she may not have intended to cause death or intended to cause any bodily injury to the child. However, the degree of knowledge and the probability of the death ensuing by the act of the accused is higher in section 300(4) where the accused must be attributed not only the knowledge of a mere probability but the knowledge that the act is *imminently dangerous and that in all probability* {not mere probability as provided in section 299(c)} that the act is likely to cause death or likely to cause such bodily injury as is likely to cause death, and that further the prosecution has to prove that there was no excuse for incurring such a risk. It will be sufficient to say that clause (4) of section 300 would be applicable where the knowledge of the offender as to the probability of death of a person or persons in general—distinguished from a particular person or persons—being caused from his imminently dangerous act approximates to an almost practical certainty. Such knowledge on the part of the offender must be of the highest degree of probability, the act having been committed by the offender without any excuse for incurring the risk of causing death or such injuries as aforesaid. The best illustrative cases explaining distinction between sections 299(c) and 300(4) are Emperor *vs* Mt Dhirajia[3] and Gyarsibai *vs* The State.[4] In the former case the accused jumped into the well along with her child, who was in her lap, in panic as her husband was following her. The accused survived but the child died. Allahabad High Court held that though the act of the accused was imminently dangerous and she ought to have known that in all probability the act of jumping into the well was likely to cause the death of the child but she had excuse and that excuse being panic or fright of the presence of her husband who was following her. Therefore, the court held her liable only for culpable homicide not amounting to murder under section 304 part-II, IPC. In the later case the court held that accused liable for murder under clause (4) of section 300 holding that her act of jumping into the well along with the children was imminently dangerous and she ought to have known that in all probability the act of jumping into the well was likely to cause the death of the children and she had no excuse as she could have escaped from the harassment at the hands of her sister-in-law even without jumping herself into the well with her three children whose death was caused by drowning. The court held that in the former case there was and in the later case there was no excuse for incurring the risk of causing the death of the children, making the accused liable for punishment under section 302, IPC.

3. AIR 1940 All. 486.
4. AIR 1953 M.B. 61.

Thus, whenever a court is confronted with the question whether the offence is 'murder' or 'culpable homicide not amounting to murder' on the facts of a case, the court must approach the problem in three stages. In the first stage, the question to be considered would be to consider whether the accused has caused the death of another. Proof of such causal connection between the act of the accused and the death, leads to the second stage for considering whether that act of the accused amounts to 'culpable homicide' as defined in section 299. If the answer to this question is *prima facie* found in the affirmative, the stage for considering the applicability of section 300, penal code, is reached. This is the stage at which the court should determine whether the facts proved by the prosecution bring the case within the ambit of any of the four clauses of the definition of 'murder' contained in section 300. If the answer to this question is in the negative the offence would be 'culpable homicide not amounting to murder' punishable under the first or second part of section 304 depending respectively on whether the second or the third clause of section 299 is applicable. If the answer to this question is found in the positive, but the case comes within any of the exceptions enumerated in section 300, the offence would still be 'culpable homicide not amounting to murder' punishable under the first part of section 304, penal code. If the case of the accused falls in section 300 and is not covered in any of the exceptions to section 300, the offence committed by the accused is murder punishable under section 302 IPC. These are only broad guidelines and not cast-iron imperatives.

In *Abdul Waheed Khan*[5] the accused, with the object to rob the deceased and if necessary, by eliminating him,

5. *Supra* note 3.

waited near the deceased's house armed with knives. The accused attacked the deceased as soon as he came out of his car giving him indiscriminate stab injuries with their knives and one of the accused tried to snatch the bag containing the cash and the demand drafts. When one of the bystander rushed to rescue the deceased the main accused threw chilli powder water on his face and he shouted for help. Further knife blows were given by the three accused till the deceased collapsed after which they fled with the bag containing cash and bank drafts. The post-mortem report indicated that there were six stab wounds and two of them were sufficient to cause death in the normal course of nature. The doctor opined that the cause of death could be the stab wound associated with the head injury. There was evidence of witnesses that the three appellants had indiscriminately stabbed the deceased, though their object was to rob the deceased. The accused persons had expected resistance and all of the three were armed with knives. When there was expected resistance by the deceased, they went on giving stabs with the knives till the deceased lost his life and thereafter the cash and demand drafts were snatched. The trial court convicted the accused under section 304 part-I which conviction was converted to murder under section 302 by the High Court. The question before the Supreme Court was whether the High Court was right in convicting the accused under section 300 thirdly. The court held that it is the intention that prevails at the time of assaults which determines the applicability of the relevant provisions. The court further held that totality of the circumstances and the nature of the injuries sustained by the deceased at the hands of the accused and the opinion of the doctor that the stab wounds as well as the head injury were individually sufficient to cause death had necessarily to be taken into account to determine the guilt of the accused. Applying the tests laid down in *Virsa Singh* and followed consistently thereafter for the applicability of clause thirdly, the Supreme Court held that the High Court had rightly convicted the accused under section 300(3) and punished under section 302, IPC.

The test laid down in *Virsa Singh* were also applied by the court in *Dhupa Chamar*[6] where the often raised argument was that the accused had given only one solitary blow with a *bhala* on the neck of the deceased and he could not be held guilty of murder.

The facts in Dhupa Chamar *vs* State of Bihar were that the appellant was a member of a group of persons who came armed with deadly weapons and there was an altercation and exchange of hot words whereafter the appellant assaulted the deceased with a *bhala* blow on the left side of the neck of the deceased. The *bhala* was pulled out forcibly from the neck by the appellant as a result of which important blood vessels were ruptured inasmuch as aorta and artery of the deceased were cut. The deceased fell down and died instantaneously. According to the post-mortem report the death was due to cardiac respiratory failure as a result of severe haemorrhage and shock due to the rupture of great veins referred to in the post-mortem report. The trial court convicted the appellant under section 302. The High Court upheld the conviction.

In the Supreme Court the appellant argued that his conviction under section 302, IPC was unwarranted as he had inflicted a single blow on the deceased. The question before the Supreme Court was whether section 300 thirdly could be attracted when death is caused by a single blow. The court after referring to the ingredients of section 300

6. (2002) 6 SCC 506.

thirdly authoritatively enunciated in *Virsa Singh* and reiterated in post *Virsa Singh* judgments held that on examination of the facts of the present case clause thirdly of section 300 was fully attracted in view of the nature of the injury whereby important blood vessels were ruptured and also keeping in view the expert medical opinion it could be reasonably inferred therefrom that such a solitary injury inflicted on the deceased was sufficient to cause death in the ordinary course of nature. The court held that in the absence of evidence or reasonable explanation to show that the appellant did not intend to inflict the injury by bhala in the neck with that degree of force sufficient to rupture important blood vessels and cutting of aorta and other artery, it would be perverse to conclude that he did not intent to inflict the injury that he did. The ingredient of intention to cause the said bodily injury having been established the offence would be murder as the intended injury was sufficient in the ordinary course of nature to cause death. Therefore, the inevitable conclusion was that the appellant had committed the offence of murder and not culpable homicide not amounting to murder.

II. When Homicide is caused by rash or negligent act not amounting to culpable homicide punishable under section 304-A, IPC as explained below:

   (a) A rash act involves advertent negligence. Advertent negligence or rashness means where the offender does an act or illegally omits to do which he bound under law to do knowing that it may result in death but hoping that it will not result so but it results because he knowingly lacked in care and caution expected of him as a reasonable man and was indifference to the consequences of his act or illegal omission.

A negligent act involves inadvertent negligence. Inadvertent negligence means that the accused has neither criminal intent nor knowledge while doing the act or omitting to do something which he is bound in law to do and death results because of the lack of care and attention expected of him as a prudent member of the society.

Homicide resulting from advertent or inadvertent culpable negligence is punishable under section 304A of the Indian Penal Code (IPC). It is important to state here that rash or negligent homicide is punishable because culpable negligence, whether advertent or inadvertent, is treated as a form of guilty mind (*mens rea*) and an act or illegal omission on the part of the accused amounts to an act (*actus rea*). The term 'act' under sections 32 and 33 of the IPC means a single act or a single illegal omission and also includes series of illegal acts or illegal omissions. The said mental element of rashness or negligence accompanying the act or illegal omission of the accused if results in the forbidden consequence i.e. death, the third element of the offence. Thus, the offence under section 304A providing punishment for causing death by rash or negligent act not amounting to culpable homicide conforms to the common law principle of *actus non facit reum nisi mens sit rea* having all the three elements of a crime namely *mens rea*, *actus rea* and forbidden consequence.

It would also be relevant to mention here that the 'Right to Life' has been held as the most important of all the fundamental rights granted to the citizens of the country. Article 21 of the Constitution of India very emphatically provides that "No person shall be deprived of his personal liberty except according to procedure established by law." Hon'ble Supreme Court of India in the case titled Smt Maneka Gandhi *vs* Union of India[7] further expanded the

7. (1978) 1 SCC 248.

scope of the provision of the 'Right to Life' as guaranteed in Article 21 of the Constitution and ruled that the a person should not only be deprived of his personal liberty except according to the procedure established by law but the procedure of law depriving a person his right of personal liberty must be 'just, fair and reasonable'. In the Chairman, Railway Board *vs* Mrs Chandrima Das[8] the Apex Court has ruled that the Constitutional rights under Article 21, that is 'Right to Life', are available even to the non-citizens also. Death of an offender in the course of police action, therefore, has to be to be properly justified, lest it will amount to the violation of the fundamental right 'Right to Life' guaranteed by the Constitution and can also amount to commission of the offences even of murder.

The provisions contained in the Constitution of India, Indian Penal Code, 1861 and the Criminal Procedure Code, 1973 make it clear that law does not authorize police to use force to the extent of killing even an armed offender except under certain situations arising at the time of face off with an armed offender. Such situation may arise either during arrest of the armed offender resisting his arrest by the police, or an armed offender attacking the police personnel—police being the visible authority of the State—as often happens in terrorism affected areas. Depending upon the facts and circumstances of the case, killing in a police action, which is a homicide, would be an offence of culpable homicide amounting/not amounting to murder punishable under section 302 of the IPC, or section 304 part 1 of the IPC, or section 304 part 2 of the IPC, as the case may be, unless it is justified by the police within the framework of general exceptions contained in

8. (2000) 2 SCC 465.

part IV of IPC including the Right of Private Defence. Further, death of a person resulting due to rash or negligent act of the police personnel during the course of an operation can be punishable under section 304A of the IPC also.

Killing of an armed offender, which results from the use of force by the police against the armed offender, can be justified by the police only on two accounts; one, if the death of the offender was caused during the use of force by the police against an offender—accused of an offence punishable with death or with imprisonment for life—during the course of arrest if such person forcibly resisted the endeavour to arrest him, or attempted to evade the arrest (as has been provided in Section 46 of the Criminal Procedure Code, 1973), or, if the death of the offender was caused in action by police wherein the police personnel used force in exercise of the Right of Private Defence as provided under Chapter IV of the Indian Penal Code, 1860.

Right of Private Defence

The Right of Private Defence is available for protection against apprehended unlawful aggression and not for punishing the aggressor for the offence committed by him. It is a preventive and not punitive right. The right to punish for the commission of offences vests in the State (which has a duty to maintain law and order).[9] Right to Punish does not lie with private individuals or with police or with paramilitary forces or even armed forces but only through the judicial process and under rule of law. The law relating to Right of Private Defence is contained in section 96 to 105 of IPC in Chapter IV of the Act.

Section 96 does not define the expression 'Right of Private Defence'. It merely indicates that nothing is an offence which has been done in the exercise of 'Right of Private Defence'.

9. Deo Narain *vs* State of UP (1973) 1 SCC 347: AIR 1973 SC 473.

Section 97 deals with subject matter of the private defence which comprises of right to protect the body or property of (i) the persons exercising the right or (ii) of any other person. The right may be utilized in the case of every offence or attempt to commit any offence against the human body, and in case of offence of theft, robbery, mischief or criminal trespass and attempts to commit such offences in relation to property. Section 99 laid down the limits of the Right of Private Defence. Sections 96 and 98 give a Right of Private Defence against certain offences and acts. The rights given in sections 96 to 98 and 100 to 106 are controlled by section 99. The Right of Private Defence extends to voluntarily causing of death subject to the limitations laid down in section 99 and other related provisions. The accused must show that there were circumstances giving rise to reasonable grounds for apprehending that either death or grievous heart or any other offence enumerated under section 100 would be caused to him and causing of death was necessary in such circumstances. Section 100 of the IPC provides that the Right of Private Defence of the body extends even to the voluntary causing of death if the offence which occasions the exercise of the right be such an assault as may reasonably cause the apprehension that death will otherwise be the consequence of such assault; an assault as may reasonably cause the apprehension that grievous hurt will otherwise be the consequence of such assault; an assault with the intention of committing rape; an assault with the intention of gratifying unnatural lust; an assault with the intention of kidnapping or abducting; and, an assault with the intention of wrongfully confining a person, under circumstances which may reasonably cause him to apprehend that he will be unable to have recourse to the public authorities for his release.

Similarly, section 103 of the IPC provides that force can be used to the extent of even causing death of the offender if the offender commits or attempts to commit an offence of robbery, house-breaking by night, mischief by fire committed on a human dwelling or as a place for custody of property, and theft, mischief, or house-trespass, under such circumstances as may reasonably cause apprehension that death or grievous hurt will be the consequence, if such Right of Private Defence is not exercised.

Thus in the context of a police operation while exercising the Right of Private Defence of the Body the police can use force even to the extent of killing the offender only if the offender indulges in "such an assault as may reasonably cause the apprehension that death or grievous hurt will otherwise be consequence of such assault."

As stated above, right to use force in self-defence is however not an absolute right; it is subjected to restrictions under the scheme of law provided in the IPC. Section 99 of the IPC puts a limit on the extent to which force can be used during exercise of the Right of Private Defence and provides that "the Right of Private Defence in no case extends to the inflicting of more harm than it is necessary to inflict for the purpose of defence". Thus, under the Right of Private Defence the police do not have the unlimited right to use force to any extent when faced with the armed offender offering resistance to the police. Section 99 thus prohibits excessive use of force during a police operation and requires use of force which is commensurate with the imminent threat that the police officer may reasonably apprehend during the operation.

The burden is on the accused to show that he had Right of Private Defence which extended to causing of death. Sections 100 and 101 define the limit and extent of Right of Private Defence. Sections 102 and 105 deal with commencement and continuation of Right of Private Defence of Body and Property respectively. The right commences, as soon as, a reasonable apprehension of the danger to the body arises from an attempt or threat to commit the offence, although the offence may not have been committed and lasts till such reasonable apprehension last.

In Rizan *vs* State of Chhattisgarh[10], the court observed that the question whether a person acted in exercise of Right of Private Defence is dependent on surrounding circumstances of the case. The court held that it is also well settled that it is not necessary for the accused to plead in so many words that he acted in self-defence. If the circumstances show that Right of Private Defence was legitimately exercised, it is open to the court to consider such a plea. In a given case the court can consider it even if the accused has not taken such a plea but such a conclusion is discernible from the available material on record. Under section 105 of the Indian Evidence Act, 1872 the burden of proof is on the accused, who sets off the plea of self-defence, and, in the absence of proof, it is not possible for the court to presume the truth of the plea of self-defence. The court shall presume the absence of such circumstances. An accused taking the plea of Right of Private Defence is not required to call evidence; he can establish his plea by reference to the circumstances transpiring from the prosecution evidence itself. The question in such a case would be a question of assessing the true effect of the prosecution evidence, and not a question of the accused discharging any burden. Where the Right of Private Defence is pleaded, the defence must be a reasonable and probable version satisfying the court that the harm caused by the accused was necessary for either warding off the attack or for forestalling the further reasonable apprehension from the side of the accused. The burden of establishing the plea of self-defence stands discharged by showing preponderance of probabilities in favour of that plea on the basis of material on record.

---

10. (2003) 2 SCC 661.

Further, often a tendency is noted that the policemen during a police operation open fire upon the offender merely upon seeing him carrying a firearm, anticipating that the armed offender would open fire upon them. Position in law regarding commencement of use of force in exercise of right to private defence is—since firing by the police personnel during the course of a police operation is resorted to in exercise of the Right of Private Defence—that the use of force in exercise of Right of Private Defence of the Body commences only when a reasonable apprehension of danger to the body arises from an attempt or threat to commit the offence though the offence may not have been committed; and it continues as long as such apprehension of danger to the body continues (section 102 of the IPC). Therefore, during a police operation force cannot be used against the armed offender merely upon noticing that the offender is armed with fire arms.

Similarly, section 105 of the IPC provides that the use of force in exercise of Right of Private Defence of Property commences when a reasonable apprehension of danger to the property commences. This section also provides that the Right of Private Defence of Property against theft continues till the offender has effected his retreat with the property or either the assistance of the public authorities is obtained, or the property has been recovered; the Right of Private Defence of Property against robbery continues as long as the offender causes or attempts to cause to any person death or hurt or wrongful restraint or as long as the fear of instant death or of instant hurt or of instant personal restraint continues; the Right of Private Defence of Property against criminal trespass or mischief continues as long as the offender continues in the commission of criminal trespass or mischief; and the Right of Private Defence of Property against house-breaking by night continues as long as the house-trespass which has been begun by such house-breaking continues.

In a police operation when an armed offender offers resistance and uses force against police, killing of the offender in police action can be justified if the death of the offender takes place under the circumstances wherein the police uses force in exercise of Right of Private Defence satisfying the above discussed provisions of law related to the exercise of Right of Private Defence. If the above conditions are not satisfied, the plea to use force in exercise of Right of Private Defence cannot be successfully taken by the police in case of death of the offender and under these situations the killing may amount to an offence of culpable homicide.

It would also be pertinent to mention here that the Right of Private Defence is a preventive right; it is not a punitive right. Thus, in a police operation, firing by the police on a fleeing offender, which may be inferred by presence of firearm injuries only on the back of the deceased offender, cannot be justified to have been done in exercise of the Right of Private Defence. Further, it should also be remembered that the criminal background of the deceased offender, that he was involved in many heinous cases or, that he was a 'rewardee' criminal, is not material in any manner. Criminal background of an offender does not give the police the right to kill an offender even if armed. What matters is the manner and the circumstances under which he was killed in the action by the police; whether it was in exercise of private defence by the police or under the circumstances as provided in section 46 of the CrPC.

In the absence of proper justification of killing of an offender by a police, the police party can have criminal liability for the following offences:

1. **Offence under section 302 of the IPC:** This is likely in case of a killing in a 'fake' police operation only; in cases wherein an offender has been killed by the police party

after his arrest and the police gave it a colour of a killing during a police operation. Except for this situation, a police party cannot be ordinarily held liable for an offence under section 302 of the IPC in a genuine police operation where the police fired presumably in exercise of Right of Private Defence.

2. **Offence under section 304 part I of the IPC:** Police can be held liable for having committed the offence under section 304 part I of the IPC if during the police operation an armed offender offers resistance to the police and the offender is killed in the firing by the police in the exercise of the Right of Private Defence of Person or Property, but the police exceeded the power given to them by law in exercising such Right of Private Defence (as provided in exception (ii) of the section 300 of the IPC), or, if during the face off with the offender the offender gets killed in the firing by the police, exceeding the powers given to them by law, by doing an act which the police, in good faith, believed to be lawful and necessary for the due discharge of their duty without ill-will towards the person whose death is caused (as provided in exception (iii) of the section 300 of the IPC).
3. **Offence under section 304 part II of the IPC:** Police can be liable for having committed the offence under section 304 part II of the IPC if during the operation for arrest of an offender the police personnel behaved in a rash manner and opened fire without justification which resulted in killing of the offender or any other civilian.
4. **Offence under section 304-A of the IPC:** Police can be held liable for having committed the offence under section 304-A of the IPC if during the operation for arrest of an offender, death of the offender or any other person is

caused due to a rash and negligent act by a police personnel; for example, an offender, who was unarmed and also did not offer any resistance to the police, or a civilian present in the area, got killed due to firing by a police personnel which was resorted to without taking due care and caution. Similarly, a police party may be held liable for negligence if any unexploded explosive materials such as hand grenades used during the operation, either by the police party or by the terrorist, if not detected and if remain at the spot after the operation, results in killing of the civilians who visit the site after the police left, for clearing the area.

However, the police can get some immunity or protection in the event of an unjustified killing in case of applicability of an Act like Jammu and Kashmir Disturbed Areas Act, 1992. Section 4 of the said Act provides that "in a 'disturbed area', any Magistrate or Police Officer not below the rank of Sub-Inspector or Head Constable in case of the Armed Branch of the Police may, if he is of opinion that it is necessary so to do for the maintenance of public order, after giving such due warning, as he may consider necessary, fire upon, or otherwise use force, even to the causing of death, against any person who is indulging in any act which may result in serious breach of public order or is acting in contravention of any law or order for the time being in force, prohibiting the assembly of five or more persons or the carrying of weapons or of things capable of being used as weapons or of fire arms, ammunition or explosive substances." Section 6 of the Act also provides that "in a 'disturbed area', any Magistrate or Police Officer not below the rank of a Sub-Inspector may, if he is of the opinion that it is necessary so to do, destroy any arms dump, prepared or fortified position of shelter from which aimed attacks are made or are likely to be made or are attempted to be made or any structure used as a training camp for armed volunteers or utilised as a hideout by armed gangs or absconders wanted for any offence".

The above discussion shows that killing of an offender in a police operation can be justified mainly on the grounds that use of force by the police, which resulted into death of the offender, was in exercise of the Right of Private Defence, whether of body, or of property. In the absence of a sound justification of a killing in police action the police personnel would be liable for having committed the offence of culpable homicide/ murder.

A relevant point comes here, as to at what stage—whether during the investigation or during the trial of the case—the plea of the police using force in exercise of the Right of Private Defence can be raised and established, so as to absolve the police party of being guilty of committing the offence of culpable homicide. In this context it would be relevant to quote section 105 of the Indian Evidence Act, 1872 which prescribes that "when a person is accused of any offence, the burden of proving the existence of circumstances bringing the case within any of the General Exceptions in the Indian Penal Code or within any special exception or proviso contained in any other part of the same Code, or in any law defining the offence, is upon him, and the court shall presume the absence of such circumstances". However the general practice is that during investigation of the case involving killing itself the police personnel involved in the action take plea of exercising their Right of Private Defence justifying the use of force and the final report in the case is submitted to the court proving offences against the deceased offender, mainly under section 307 of the IPC.

This issue was discussed by the Hon'ble High Court of Andhra Pradesh in the case titled Andhra Pradesh Civil Liberties Committee *vs* The Government of Andhra Pradesh in the writ petition Nos: 15419 of 2006; 26358 of 1999; 7906 of 2000; 14475 of 2002; 440 of 2003 and 857 of 2008. In the instant case the High Court in its judgment dated 6th February 2009[11] held that "where a police officer causes death of a person, acting or purporting to act in discharge of official duties or in self-defence as the case may be, the first information relating to such circumstance (even when by a Police/Public Official; whether an alleged perpetrator is named or not) shall be recorded and registered as FIR, enumerating the relevant provisions of Law, (u/s 154(1) CrPC) and shall be investigated (u/s 156/157 CrPC)" and "that the existence of circumstances bringing a case within any of the Exceptions in the Indian Penal Code including the exercise of the Right of Private Defence (a General Exception in Chapter IV IPC), cannot be conclusively determined during investigation. The opinion recorded by the Investigating Officer in the final report forwarded to the Magistrate (u/s 173 CrPC), is only an opinion. Such opinion shall be considered by the Magistrate in the context of the record of investigation together with the material and evidence collected during the course of investigation. The Magistrate (notwithstanding an opinion of the Investigating Officer, that no cognizable offence appears to have been committed; that one or more or all of the accused are not culpable; or that the investigation discloses that the death of civilian(s) in a police operation is not culpable in view of legitimate exercise by the police of the Right of Private Defence), shall critically examine the entirety of the evidence collected during investigation to ascertain whether the opinion of the Investigating Officer is borne out by the record of investigation. The Magistrate has the discretion to disregard the opinion and take cognizance of the offence u/s 190 CrPC."

---

11. Available at the website: https://docs.google.com/document/d/1PDZl gpCSYLcKipid9yHDNWKnsjO85Ml9O43XcfgLSD8/edit?pli=1

Thus, in view of this judgment it would be compulsory for the police to register an FIR against the police officers after every police operations resulting in death of an offender. It had also ruled that their plea of self-defence should be considered by the judicial magistrate only after the Investigating Officer had filed his final report. However, on an appeal filed by the Andhra Pradesh Police Officers Association, the Hon'ble Supreme Court has stayed the verdict of the High Court and the case is under consideration in the Hon'ble Supreme Court.

CHAPTER 3

Investigation of Killings in Police Operations

A genuine police operation resulting in killing of a dreaded terrorist or a criminal is generally considered a 'good work' by the police. The police party, after the successful operation feel relaxed as in the operation they also face a grave threat to their lives. After an operation resulting into killing of an offender, investigation of the case is usually conducted by a Sub-Inspector level officer. However, in most of the cases, very little importance is given to the investigation of the killing in police operation, mainly because it involves killing of an offender in a police action which is considered 'lawful' by the police officers. Further, a genuine killing of an offender in police action is usually not questioned by anyone, not even by the relatives of the deceased offender. Instead, the senior police officers praise such actions; media also usually praises the police action, projecting it as an act of bravery by the policemen, and, sometimes society even supports such police action, considering killing of the offender a good riddance.

The police officer carrying out investigation of death of an offender in a police operation usually gives it a low priority, and mostly completes the formalities required in the investigation. The police officer carrying out investigation of the killing however overlooks the fact that even a genuine killing is a homicide and investigation of the killing should properly establish that it was a lawful and justifiable homicide. The lacunas, left out during the investigation of the case involving killing of an armed offender, trouble the police party when at a later stage, in many instances, after considerable lapse of time, the killing is examined in judicial or quasi-judicial proceedings. Police personnel have to often face these proceedings, sometimes initiated by those having vested interest or by the upper ground network of the terrorists to harass the police. Such situations are often seen in an insurgency/Naxalite/terrorism affected areas. Therefore, investigation of a case involving killing of an offender in a police operation should be given the same importance and professionally dealt with, as is done in any other homicide case, for example in a normal murder case involving killing of a civilian.

An investigation into the death of an offender resulting from use of force by the police should clearly establish the following facts in order to give complete legitimacy to the police action during the operation:

(i) that the force used by the police, which resulted into killing of the armed offender was used by the police in exercise of 'Right of Private Defence';

(ii) that sufficient warning was given by the police to the armed offender to surrender before start of use of force by the police in exercise of the Right of Private Defence; and

(iii) that the force used by the police in exercise of Right of Private Defence was only to the extent of inflicting of such harm as was necessary to inflict for the purpose of defence. In other words, it is to be proved that only minimum required force, and not excessive force, was used by the police personnel during the incident.

The fact that police used force, which resulted into killing of the armed offender, was used by the police in exercise of the

Right of Private Defence, in addition to other evidences such as evidences by the eyewitnesses and nature and position of the wounds on the dead body of the killed offender, etc can be proved to a great extent by the following:

1. The facts that the weapons seized from the possession of the deceased offender was in working condition, that the weapons had been fired, and that the empty cartridges seized from the site of the incident were fired from the weapon seized from the possession, are strong indicators that the armed offender used the firearms against the police.
2. Matching of the fingerprints of the deceased and fingerprints on the weapons seized from the site of the incident would be strong scientific evidence that the weapons seized from the possession of the deceased offender or seized from the site of the incident were used by the offender against the police. Similarly fingerprints on the other articles/materials used by the armed offenders, such as fingerprints on the body of the vehicles used by the offenders, would also have strong evidentiary values supporting the police version.
3. Presence of gun powder residue in the hand-wash of the deceased offender would be strong scientific evidence that the deceased offender had fired a weapon in the incident in which the police used force.

Scientific evidences as mentioned above are particularly important if the incident has taken place in a remote desolate place where there is no independent civilian witness to the incident.

In view of the legal provisions, especially those contained in the Indian Penal Code and the Criminal Procedure Code, the following points need to be specifically taken care of during investigation of the killings resulting from use of force by the police in an operation:

(i) A proper site plan of the place of the incident giving all the details should be prepared, clearly showing position of the police party and the armed offenders. In addition, a 'Spot Panchnama' should also be prepared, clearly describing the scene of incident.

(ii) Proper photography of the scene of crime and of the deceased should be got conducted. Photographs of the deceased should clearly show all the wounds on the body of the deceased offender as well as all the body parts to exclude presence of any torture mark, blackening or tattooing.

(iii) 'Hand wash' of the deceased offenders should be taken, preferably at the site of the incident itself, and it should be sent for forensic examination to ascertain presence of the residue of gun powder.

(iv) Finger prints of the deceased and fingerprints on the weapons seized from the site of the incident (belonging to the deceased offenders) as well as fingerprints on the other articles/materials belonging to the deceased and seized from the site of the incident should be carefully lifted and sent to the forensic expert for matching. Similarly, fingerprints on the other articles/materials belonging to the deceased and seized from the site of the incident should be carefully lifted for matching. For instance, if the offenders were on a motorcycle when intercepted by the police party, fingerprints of the offenders from the motorcycle should also be lifted.

(v) The arms and ammunition as well as the empty/spent cartridges found at the site of the incident, which were used by the armed offender against the police, should be properly seized, and should be promptly sent to a Forensic Science Laboratory (FSL) for ballistic examination in order to ascertain that the seized arms were in working condition, and that the empty cartridges were fired from the weapons seized from the site of the incident.

Delay in sending the seized arms and ammunition may result in loss of important evidences due to rusting of weapon and other possible damages. Further, sometimes ballistic examination is got done by an armourer which would however be of very little evidentiary value.

Sometimes it may also happen that the associates of the deceased armed offender take away weapon of the deceased and only empty cases/spent cartridges are recovered from the spot. In this situation, the weapons used by the police should be sent for ballistic examination to establish that the empty cases seized from the site of the incident were not fired by the police weapon used in the operation.

(vi) Clothes of the deceased offender, especially those having bullet marks, should be forensically examined for presence of gunpowder and other depositions associated with firing as it can give an indication of range of firing.

(vii) In case a police vehicle or the vehicle used by the offenders got damaged during the operation or was hit by a bullet, this fact should be properly brought on record. Photographs showing damages to the vehicle should be taken and the vehicle should be properly got examined by the Motor Vehicle Inspector.

Further, all the records in connection with the use of force resulting in killing of the offender during the operation should be properly prepared. The police party, before going out for the operation should make an appropriate entry in the General Diary of the Police Station. Similarly, on return after the operation, a detailed account of the incident should be entered in the General Diary and other records of the police station. Senior police officers who led the police team during the operation should themselves lodge the First Information Report (FIR), clearly bringing out relevant facts and circumstances of the incident, particularly those which necessitated use of force by the police in exercise of Right of Private Defence, injury to any police personnel during the incident, damage to any vehicle, seizure of arms and ammunition and spent cartridges and number of rounds fired by the by the police party. Seizure of the arms/ammunition, spent cases, blood-stained earth sample and other relevant evidences from the spot should be effected following appropriate procedures, and a proper seizure memo indicating names and signature of the witnesses—preferably independent witnesses, date and time of the seizure, etc should be prepared. The Investigating Officer should make a proper entry in the General Diary of the Police Station regarding action taken by him such as seizure of arms/ammunition, empty cases and other articles, taking of hand wash, taking of fingerprints, conducting photography, identification of the dead criminal (identified by whom and how) and handing over of the dead body to the relatives of the deceased, etc. During the course of investigation the Investigating Officer should collect all the evidences which are relevant to prove genuineness of the circumstances leading to use of force by the police.

Importance of proper investigation and other relevant aspects related to a death in police action, as brought out in the cases decided by the National Human Rights Commission, can be seen as discussed below.

1. NHRC Case Number 5/16/2006-2007

1. In this case the complainants, office bearers of Mizoram Bru Displaced People's Forum, made a joint complaint to the Commission on 29th April 2006 regarding the killing of one Joinobari Reeng, aged 30 years, on 16th March 2006 by the IRP (Indian Reserve Police) personnel near Dilvi river where he was allegedly taken by 4 persons who were also alleged to be IRP personnel.
2. Pursuant to the notice of the Commission, the Director General of Police, Mizoram submitted a report that on 16th March 2006 at 1130 hours, an unidentified Bru armed with country made gun, suspected to be a BLFM cadre, was shot dead by patrolling party of 1st Bn of IRP near the Mizoram Tripura border inside Mizoram during patrolling operation by the IRP personnel on receiving information that suspected armed insurgents were seen near the Tripura border. On seeing and calling to stop they started to flee and one of them fired on the police party. Acting in self-defence police also returned back the fire in which one of them died who was later on identified as Joinobar Reeng. He was in possession of a weapon which resembled with AK-47 rifle. Concerning the incident a case crime No 3/06 u/s 307/189/506/34 IPC r/w 25/30 Arms Act was registered. Other fleeing insurgents were also identified.
3. The Commission noted that no magisterial enquiry was held in this incident, despite its guidelines. However, the Commission received the post-mortem examination report as well as a detailed report prepared by the police. The police party concerned claimed that they had an exchange of fire with some men whom they described as members of an insurgent group. After this encounter, which took place around 11.30 AM, they recovered a gun from the person of Joinbar Reeng and, as reported by them, they went home

leaving the body and reported the incident to officer in-charge Zawlnuam. The body was retrieved on the same night. The Commission noted from the post-mortem examination report that the late Joinbar Reeng was hit by only one bullet, which entered the right buttock and emerged from the inguinal region. This wound would not have been fatal, and, as the doctors who conducted the autopsy noted, the cause of death was 'shock due to excessive bleeding'. The Commission observed that "it is certain that the policemen who shot Joinbar Reeng would have found him alive when they recovered the weapon from him. It is also clear from their own reports that they made no effort to get him medical attention, which was their duty. Instead, in an act of the utmost cruelty, they left him there to bleed to death. This was a most grievous violation of human rights". The Commission therefore asked the Government of Mizoram to 'show cause' why it should not recommend relief for the next of kin of the late Joinbar Reeng.

4. In response to its show cause notice, the Commission received a reply from the Government of Mizoram, in which the State claimed that the late Joinbar Reeng 'lost his life in the exchange of fire with the patrolling party', that 'the patrolling party had rightly discharged its legal duties', and that therefore 'there was no violation of human rights on the part of the State Police Force'.

5. The Commission however, did not accept this contention and observed as under:

> "It is clear from the nature of the injury established in the post-mortem that Joinbar Reeng would not have died instantly. He was shot on his right buttock, and the postmortem noted that all his internal organs were healthy. **No vital organ having been hit by the bullet,**

Joinbar Reeng would have survived if he had been given immediate medical care. However, the police party, according to the report sent by the SDPO, all admitted that they went home after the alleged encounter. It was this negligence that led to the death of Joinbar Reeng. The police claim that he was dead when they abandoned him, but only a qualified medical practitioner could have declared him dead, and the Commission reiterates that he would not have died instantly from the injury that he received. The inquest was conducted on him at 9.20 PM, though the encounter took place at 11.30 AM. It is clear, therefore, that no attention was given to him for almost 10 hours, though, when a person is injured, it is the duty of the police to ensure that he receives prompt medical attention. This callous negligence of the policemen involved led to a death, and was therefore the most grievous violation of human rights. The Commission notes that the State also claims that Joinbar Reeng died in an exchange of fire, which he initiated. However, that has not been established by any scientific or forensic evidence. In any professional criminal investigation, the Commission would have expected the police to conduct tests and furnish reports that would have established that fingerprints on the weapon recovered matched those of the dead man; confirmed from ballistic tests that the gun was in working order, had been recently fired, and that spent ammunition recovered from the site matched it; and shown that forensic tests on swabs for gunshot residue taken from the fingers of the deceased proved that he had recently fired a weapon. The absence of any of these tests means either that the investigation was not professionally conducted, or that this was a deliberate decision to mask the truth. In either case, in the absence of this evidence, there is nothing to substantiate the claim made by the patrol that Joinbar Reeng had fired at them."

6. The Commission, therefore, did not accept the response of the Government of Mizoram. It maintained its view that a grievous violation of human rights was committed by the policemen involved, and recommended to the Government of Mizoram to pay ₹ 5 lakh as relief for the next of kin of the late Joinbar Reeng. This recommendation of the Commission was accepted by the Government of Mizoram.

2. NHRC Case Number 10/3/2005-2006 (Linked with case number 16/3/2005-2006)

1. Sr DISPOL City, Guwahati, Assam sent information to the Commission regarding the death of an unidentified person in a police encounter on 1st April 2005. It was intimated that in the intervening night of 1-2 April 2005, while a police party was conducting search at Chandannagar to apprehend the militants involved in the incident of lobbing of grenade at Ganesguri Chariali, police team noticed a group of some three-four persons moving in suspicious manner. When they were commanded to halt for their identification, they suddenly opened fire at the police personnel and injured one constable. Police also fired upon them for self-defence. When the firing stopped, one unidentified youth was found dead at the place of incident. A case FIR No 428/2005 u/s 120(B)/121(A)/122/353/326/307/511 IPC r/w Section 27(2) Arms Act r/w Section 4/5 ES Act was registered in the matter in PS Dispur.
2. Pursuant to the directions of the Commission, IGP (OSD), In-Charge, Human Rights Cell, Assam Police sent

report to the Commission mentioning that investigation of the case FIR number 428/2005 of PS Dispur was conducted by the CID in accordance with the guidelines of the NHRC. During investigation, no other co-accused could be identified except one who was also released in absence of sufficient evidences.

3. From scrutiny of the report the Commission observed that the incident took place in the intervening night of 01-02/04/2005 at about 1.10 AM and there were no eye-witnesses to the incident. The deceased was having hand grenade on his person, and one walkie-talkie, two electronic detonators and 12 empty cases of bullets were also found at the place of incident but no firearm could be found at the scene of crime or on person. Therefore, one could assume that deceased did not injure the constable by firing upon him. Further, the post-mortem report revealed the cause of death as a result of head injury and that all the injuries were caused by fire arm except the injury in the abdomen which was caused by blunt object. The post-mortem report also revealed that all the injuries were anti-mortem and homicidal in nature. However, how the deceased sustained blunt injuries in abdomen or the nature and the gravity of that injury was not clear from the report. The Commission also noted that the police report mentioned that "the prime accused of the case died and the others escaped. Their identity could not be traced out and there is no hope of tracing out the miscreants in the near future." However, how police reached at this conclusion that the deceased was the prime accused of the case and what efforts were made by the police to trace the other co-accused was not revealed in the police report. The Commission, therefore, directed the DGP, Assam to submit Magisterial Enquiry Report (MER) and inquest report of the deceased.

4. Pursuant to the directions of the Commission the District Magistrate, Kamrup sent a copy of the inquest, post-mortem examination report and a brief magisterial enquiry report. The inquest and post-mortem examination report revealed 26 fire arm and other type of injuries on the body of the deceased. The cause of death was recorded as due to the injuries described in the post-mortem report. The post-mortem report also revealed that all the injuries were caused by fire arm except injury in the abdomen which was caused by blunt object. All the injuries were ante-mortem and homicidal in nature and the death was caused within 12 to 18 hours of the post-mortem examination. The post-mortem examination appeared to have been done on 4th May 2005. The SDM, Kamrup in the magisterial enquiry report did not express any inference or finding regarding the veracity of the police encounter. He simply mentioned that death of the deceased was caused due to bullet injury during the course of encounter with the militants.
5. The Commission noted that the "police encounter is reported to be held on 1/2 April 2005 while the post-mortem report reveals that death was caused within 12-18 hours of the time of post-mortem examination. The post-mortem examination was done on 4th May 2005. Thus, on the said inference the death of the deceased should not have been caused due to said operation and encounter with militants. Therefore, it is necessary that a fresh magisterial enquiry be ordered into the death of the deceased for ascertaining as to whether the deceased died during the said operation and encounter with militants."
6. In the light of the aforesaid observations the Commission recommended to the DM, Kamrup to order fresh magisterial enquiry into the death of the deceased associating the

local inhabitants and submit the Magisterial Enquiry report to the Commission. The Commission also recommended to the Secretary Home, Government of Assam to order investigation into the aforesaid case crime No 428/05 Police Station (PS) Dispur by the CB/CID (Crime Branch/ Criminal Investigation Department).

7. In response to the Commission's direction, a second Magisterial Enquiry Report and the report of the SSP (CID) Assam on the death of Dip Sarmah was received in the Commission. Both confirmed the finding of the first Magisterial Enquiry Report that Dip Sarmah was killed in a genuine encounter with the police when he, together with other accomplices, had fired and thrown grenades at the police party that had challenged them.

8. Having examined these documents, the Commission observed that there were several questions that had troubling connotations. First, according to both the police report as well as that of the inquest, the body of the deceased was found clutching a live grenade in the right hand. However, the post-mortem report showed that two bullets hit him on his right arm and right elbow. It would have been very difficult for someone hit by two rifle bullets in his right arm to be able to hold on to anything. Secondly, if it was accepted that the deceased was able to retain his hold on the grenade, the inquest, held about seven hours after the encounter took place, found that rigor mortis had set in, which would be normal. An object held in the fingers of a body with established rigor mortis could not be removed except with specialized procedures. However, there was nothing in the inquest, police or post-mortem reports to show that any such procedure was undertaken. In the circumstances, it was difficult to see how a live grenade could have been safely removed. Thirdly, though the body

was described in both the inquest and the post-mortem report as that of an unidentified male, according to the SDM, Kamrup it was identified on the 2nd April 2005 around 6.30 PM by the deceased's brother, Shri Sailen Sarmah of Tihu Natun Baniakuchi in Nalbari district. This meant that the identification took place within 15 hours of the death. However, since the village where the brother lived was at the farthest extremity of a district that adjoined Kamrup, it needed to be explained how he came to know of his brother's death. Lastly, though the police claimed that the deceased was accompanied by others who escaped under the cover of darkness and using the cover of buildings where the encounter took place, the Magistrate recorded that at the time of the incident this place was open, and the habitation now seen were 'recent developments'. This was confirmed in the post-mortem report, which described the place of occurrence as an 'oxen field'. The Commission observed that the excuse given by the police was therefore not credible. **The Commission also noted that all the bullets hit the deceased from the back, which showed that when he was shot he was trying to run away from the police, not either firing or throwing grenades at them.** The Commission therefore directed the Government of Assam to provide explanations on these points. The Commission also directed to send a copy of the treatment record of the constable Apurba Baruah, who was reportedly injured in this incident.

9. Except the answer about the injury sustained by the police personnel, the Commission found it difficult to agree with any of the propositions propounded by the State Government in its responses. In the response sent by the Government of Assam, there was a reference of "carefully removed the hand grenade from the deceased

in presence of senior officers". However, no time was mentioned. The inquest which was performed on the next day i.e. on 2nd April 2007 at 0850 hours, the grenade was found in the hand of the deceased and by that time rigor mortis had set in. The autopsy report made it very clear that there was nothing in the hand. There was nothing to indicate that the rigor mortis on the hand was broken. Therefore, the Commission observed that the explanation was given just for the sake of rendering the explanation. The Commission also found it difficult to believe the explanation about the arrival of the brother of the deceased. Under the circumstances, the Commission gave one more opportunity to the Government of Assam to properly clarify the questions raised so as to satisfy that the version of the police was correct.

10. The Commission considered the replies given by the Government of Assam to the queries of the Commission and observed that the replies were not at all in consonance with the scientific evidence and also there was no explanation on certain aspects. The Commission had earlier pointed out that the person who sustained bullet injuries had two injuries by gun shot on his right arm and right elbow. If the injuries had been caused by firearm, looking to the nature indicated in the post-mortem report, it was practically impossible for a person to keep an article in his hand. Therefore, the theory propounded by the State was difficult to believe. The State Government gave reply to a further question stating that the Professor and Head of Department of Forensic Medicines, Guwahati Medical College and the Directorate, FSL, Assam Guwahati were consulted and they opined that the grenade could be removed from the clutch of the deceased with great amount of

force, and that the Investigating Officer might have applied sufficient force to remove the said grenade. The Commission observed that "there is much distance between 'may' and 'must' and it is not known whether the Investigating Officer had applied sufficient force for removal of the said grenade or not. Merely by saying that he might have applied force is no answer'. It was also noted that according to the post-mortem report there was complete setting of rigor mortis, and it did not indicate that rigor mortis was broken at any place, particularly in the right hand. The Commission noted that "if after a long period force is used, the rigor mortis is bound to break at that place and would have been noticed by the Medical Officer. That is not the case and, therefore, the State cannot proceed on the basis of presumptions and conjectures'. **The Commission also noted that most of the injuries were on the back of the person and the indiscriminate firing showed that the police was keen to kill the person. In the aforesaid circumstances, the excessive firing which caused 26 injuries on the person of the deceased, in itself was sufficient to say that it was in violation of human rights, particularly, when most of the injuries were found on the back of the persons, meaning thereby that the injuries must have been sustained while the person was trying to run away from the police.** The Commission therefore, issued a notice u/s 18 of the Protection of Human Rights Act, 1993, to the Government of Assam to show-cause why monetary relief should not be recommended to be paid to the next of kin of the deceased Dip Sarmah.

11. In response to the 'show cause notice' the State Government forwarded opinion of a forensic expert who

pointed out about the time of onset of rigor mortis, that it begins in 1 to 2 hours after death and takes further 1 to 2 hours to develop, and that it usually lasts for 24 to 48 hours in winter and 18 to 36 hours in summer while it lasts for 2 to 3 days in temperate regions. The paragraph under the heading 'Cadaveric Spasm or Instanteneous Rigor' mentioned that "This is a phenomenon in which the muscles that have been in a state of contraction during life become stiff and rigid immediately after death without passing into an initial state of relaxation; hence the attitude of the body adopted at the time of death is maintained for several hours till rigor mortis develops. Generally it is restricted to single group of muscles. This occurs in cases where there have been great muscular exertion and mental excitement, before sudden death, as observed amongst soldiers killed on a battle field. In case of cadaveric spasm a weapon held in hand is firmly grasped and can only be removed with difficulty whereas in cadaveric rigidity or rigor mortis the weapons placed in the hand before rigor mortis has set in, is not grasped, but drops down from the hand on slightest touch. For practical purpose it is not possible for murderer to initiate this condition. It represents last act of life". The Commission noted that this opinion, on the contrary, suggested that it could not have been possible to remove the grenade without breakage of rigor mortis. The Commission observed that the State had not satisfactorily answered the queries raised by the Commission and recommended to the State of Assam to pay a sum of ₹ 5 lakh to the next of kin of deceased Dip Sarmah. Recommendation of the Commission was accepted by the Government of Assam.

3. NHRC Case Number 1245/12/2005-2006

1. The Commission took cognizance of intimation from the Satna Police about the death of 3 dacoits in an encounter with the police on the 29th September 2005 near village Bookharwar, Satna, Madhya Pradesh. The report of SP, Satna revealed that intimation was received by the police regarding presence of dacoits near village Bookharwar in Madhya Pradesh. Acting on this information, the police party surrounded the area and warned the dacoits. The dacoits started firing indiscriminately and the police returned the fire in self-defence. The firing continued for 45 minutes in which three dacoits were killed. A case number 61/05 u/s 147/148/149/307 IPC, 25/27 of Arms Act and 9/11 Anti-Dacoity Act was registered.
2. Subsequently, the Commission received and examined, among other documents, the Magisterial Enquiry Report, the post-mortem report and the inquest report. During the Magisterial enquiry the police claimed to the Magistrate that after receiving reports that two criminal gangs, one of strength around 25 and another of strength around 12, were gathering near Bookharwar village, they formed three teams to arrest them. They reached the place around 2.30 in the afternoon and, after surrounding the criminals, asked them to surrender. Instead, the criminals opened fire and the police were forced to return fire in self-defence. The firing continued for 45 minutes. After it stopped the police found three dead bodies, one of which could not be identified. The other two were identified as the criminals Gudda @ Maiyadeen Patel, and Bhullu S/o Rishi Ram Kewat. According to the police, the other criminals escaped.
3. The post-mortem reports showed that the firearm entry wounds on all the dead bodies were blackened, which was

forensic evidence that the shots were fired at extremely close range. The Commission observed that this contradicted the account given by the police. The autopsy of the deceased who could not be identified, showed that he had a bullet wound on his left thigh, which was unlikely to have been fatal, but he also had an incised wound over his scalp caused by a hard and sharp object. The Commission also noted that, "according to the testimony of the police, they fired 250 rounds, a high volume of ammunition. However, only a very few seemed to have hit the mark. Apart from the three who were killed, over 30 other criminals seem to have escaped in broad daylight though they had, according to the police, been surrounded by three of their teams. This did not seem probable, unless the police were grossly incompetent". The Commission also noted that, "according to the police, though their teams exchanged fire for such a long time with two groups of armed criminals, not one policeman had even a scratch, which might be providential but, which, if the encounter had taken place as described, is not very probable". The Magistrate did not seem to have considered these very significant points, which called into question the credibility of the account given by the police. In the circumstances, the Commission found it hard to agree with the conclusions of the enquiry Magistrate or to give credence to the account given by the police and the Commission recommended to the Government of Madhya Pradesh to carry out an independent investigation by the CB CID.

4. The report presented by the CB CID was examined by the Investigation Division of the NHRC on the directions of the Commission. On the recommendation of the Investigation Division, the Commission directed

the CB CID to clarify whether the clothes worn by the deceased at the time of encounter were seized and sent to Ballistic expert to find whether black amorphous material and component of powder was present or not on the entrance of the wounds.

5. The CB CID's report, together with the further forensic analysis revealed that the CB CID had come to the conclusion about genuineness of the encounter for three broad sets of reasons: (i) relatives of the dead men admitted that they were criminals; (ii) the villagers who were independent witnesses had not alleged that the police had executed the men; and (iii) while the forensic examination of the clothes worn by the deceased had found traces of nitrite on some bullet holes but not on others, showing that only some shots were fired from close range, the post-mortem recorded blackening on all wounds, the inference being that this was a mistake.

6. On the first of these three contentions, the Commission accepted the police claim that the two dead men who were identified were criminals. However the Commission observed that "it is odd that the third man remains unidentified, though their accomplices, who were subsequently arrested, should have been able to name him if he was a member of the gang". **The Commission also noted that "it is not their criminal antecedents that the Commission is considering, but the circumstances in which they were killed".** The Commission further observed that the second point made by the CB CID was deliberately misleading as no villager saw the encounter; all of them stated during the magisterial enquiry that they hid when the firing started and only emerged to be shown the dead bodies after it stopped. They did not see how the men were killed.

7. Regarding the third point, which related to scientific evidence, the Commission observed as under:

   "Even a delayed examined of clothes that may well not have been carefully preserved has established the presence of nitrite, which confirms that at least some of the shots were fired from extremely close range. Since the police claimed that they exchanged fire at a distance, this proves that their testimony was false on this point. It also proves that the fatal shots were fired at close range, which is the hallmark of an execution. The Commission cannot accept the inference that, because nitrite was not detected at some of the entry wounds on the clothes, the postmortem was faulty, because it found blackening on all wounds. There are several reasons why the delayed forensic examination may not have found nitrite on all the holes on the clothes. Among these are the following: (a) forensic science makes it clear that, though nitrite is normally not wiped off, for their presence to be fully detected, the clothes to be examined need to be air-dried, and carefully preserved. There is no evidence that this was done in this case; (b) forensic science has established that different shots deposit different amounts of nitrite; it is entirely possible in this case that the shots that left a lighter residue on the clothes were now not traceable, since the examination took place after so long; (c) forensic science also notes that nitrite can sometimes be masked or washed away by a heavy flow of blood from a wound; (d) some of the shots on which blackening were found were to the skull or to the arms, which in late summer would have been bare. Therefore, while the forensic examination of the clothes confirms that some of the shots were certainly fired at contact range, the apparent absence of nitrite on some holes does not refute the evidence of the qualified surgeons who conducted the autopsy and recorded the presence of blackening on all wounds."

8. For these reasons, the Commission did not accept the findings of the CB CID. It accepted that the deceased men were criminals and it was also possible that there was an exchange of fire with the police but the evidence of the autopsy, reinforced by the examination of the clothes, confirmed that, at the end of this exchange, these three men were executed at close range.
9. The Commission held it a grievous violation of human rights and asked the Government of Madhya Pradesh to 'show cause' why it should not recommend relief for the next of kin of the late Gudda @ Maiyadeen Patel and Bhullu.
10. In response to its recommendations for relief, the Commission received a response from the Government of Madhya Pradesh in which it was argued that relief for the next of kin in this case was not justified for two reasons, that the magisterial enquiry had held that the police action was justified, and that the court has subsequently sentenced two of the criminals who had been arrested.
11. The Commission did not accept this as a substantive response as it had already explained in detail in its earlier proceedings why it was unable to expect the magisterial enquiry, which had not examined several critical points and it was for this reason that the Commission had asked the Government of Madhya Pradesh to have a further investigation carried out by the CB CID. As far as the sentencing of the two men was concerned, the

Commission observed that in its proceedings, the Commission had accepted that the man killed were indeed criminals and that it was also possible that there was an exchange of fire with the police. Therefore, the fact that a court had come to the same conclusion simply confirmed a point already accepted by this Commission. What the Commission had nevertheless found, after its initial examination and a subsequent analysis of the report of the CB CID, was that at the end of a possible exchange of fire, three men executed by the police at close range. This was not only illegal, but a grievous violation of human rights and it was for this reason that the Commission had recommended to the Government of Madhya Pradesh that relief should be given to the next of kin of the late Gudda @ Maiyadeen Patel and Bhullu. The Government of Madhya Pradesh had not answered the substantive points on the basis of which the Commission made its recommendation. Therefore, the Commission did not see any reason to reconsider its view that relief was indeed justified and necessary, and therefore recommended to the Government of Madhya Pradesh to pay ₹ 5 lakh each as relief to the next of kin of the late Gudda @ Maiyadeen Patel and Bhullu. Recommendation of the Commission was accepted by the Government of Madhya Pradesh.

4. NHRC Case No 32646/24/53/2010

1. The complainant Shri Parag in his complaint dated 7th June 2010 to the Commission alleged that on 25th May 2010 at about 7 PM police came in three vehicles and picked up his son Seshnath for interrogation along with the motorcycle from his house in village Fatehpur, district Mau, Uttar Pradesh. He was promised that after

interrogation he will be released but he did not return. On the next day he came to know through the press reports that his son had been killed in a fake encounter. Earlier, the Commission had received a complaint dated 1 June 2010 from the complainant regarding alleged illegal arrest of complainant's son Seshnath by the police. Intimation on the same subject received in the Commission from the SP, Azamgarh mentioned that Raj Srivastava and Seshnath Chauhan (son of the complainant) died in an encounter with the police in the area of police station Kotwali, district Azamgarh.

2. The Commission received a detailed report from the police, together with copies of the post-mortem and magisterial enquiry reports, but given the circumstances of the case, on which it had received a complaint from the family of the Seshnath Chauhan that the police had abducted him before the encounter, the Commission directed its Investigation Division to conduct a spot enquiry in this case.

3. Reading the documents the Commission noted that Seshnath, the deceased was not initially identified though he was involved in various crimes according to the police. Another deceased Srivastava, according to the police, was a criminal and both were together on a motorbike. But there was nothing to state positively that both were known to each other so as to indulge in a crime together. The pattern of crime followed by each was different and in the absence of any reliable material to say that they were together in the manner in which it was suggested was doubtful. The Commission also noted that in the instant case, the person who was threatened by Srivastava stated that the threatening call was given on a telephone. The police claimed that deceased Srivastava was moving with a

mobile, but there was no satisfactory evidence collected by the Investigating Agency to connect the mobile and the telephone with the person who was threatened. Police had come out with the version that on 25th May 2010 at 4.05 AM soon after the threatening call was received from Srivastava, the complainant Shri Padmakar Verma contacted the SP, who in turn deputed SHO, PS Kotwali. The Commission therefore directed the SP Azamgarh to send Xerox copy of GD entries of 24th May 2010, 25th May 2010 and 26th May 2010 along with the legible transcript and the call records collected in the instant case to establish the fact that Srivastava had a conversation with the complainant Shri Padmakar Verma.

4. On examination of these documents the Commission observed as under:

> "The first point the Commission notes is that, though Raj Srivastava was identified on the spot, Seshnath Chauhan was still unidentified when the post-mortem was conducted at 5.45 PM on the 26th May 2010. It is important to establish how he was ultimately identified, in view of the complaint received in the Commission. A comparison of the reports from the police with their statements to the magisterial enquiry and to the Commission's investigation team shows that the police of Azamgarh district have given false testimony, as the following sequence makes clear: (i) the police of Azamgarh claimed that Seshnath Chauhan's body was identified by his cousin Munna Chauhan; (ii) however, the report from the Circle Officer, Mohammadabad in district Mau, dated the 26th September 2010, made it clear that on the early afternoon of the 26th the SHO of PS Ranipur received a call from Govind Singh, SHO of PS Kotwali,

informing him that Seshnath Chauhan had been killed in an encounter, he had been identified, and his family should be informed; (iii) the SHO of PS Ranipur told the Commission's officers that he received this telephone call between 2.30 and 3 PM, and the report from the Circle Officer Mohammadabad intimates that PC Amarnath Singh was detailed at 4.05 PM to go to the village where Seshnath Chauhan's family lived; (iv) PC Amarnath has given a statement to confirm that he took Munna Chauhan with him. Munna Chauhan has confirmed this, and has said that he saw his cousin's body after the post-mortem; (v) the post-mortem, conducted at 5.45 PM, still records Seshnath Chauhan as unidentified. It is very clear from this that, though the police of PS Kotwali knew at least by 2.30 PM who Seshnath Chauhan was, they did not inform the doctor. Clearly, they wanted to establish that a member of the family had identified him. Two further conclusions flow from this. First, the police knew who Seshnath Chauhan was well before he was identified by Munna Chauhan. Secondly, they did not want to acknowledge this, because to do so would immediately confirm that he was in their custody, since that was the only way they would have known who he was. The elaborate subterfuge into which the police entered shows that they had perhaps heard that his family was lodging a complaint about his abduction, and realized that this would create complications for them. It is clear from this that the police knew who Seshnath Chauhan was well before Munna Chauhan identified him, but went to great lengths to hide this fact. The conclusion must be that he was in their custody, and if he was, the encounter could not have taken place. Since Raj Srivastava was killed in the same encounter, it must also follow that he too was in the custody of the police, and therefore the account of his death is also false. This is confirmed by the independent evidence of the post-mortem, analysed against statements given by the police. In written statements given to the Commission's officers, the policemen involved claimed that, though several shots had been fired at them by the two men, they were not hit because they were on a slope and had immediately fallen flat on the ground. They had fired while prone up the slope at the two men, who were on a height, and had exposed themselves because they had sat up to fire at them. This being the scenario described by the police, all shots that hit the two men would have travelled sharply upwards. However, the post-mortem establishes the following: (i) Raj Srivastava was hit by two bullets. One entered his right shoulder below the acromion process, exiting through the subclavian area, while the other hit below the nipple exiting through the flank. Both, therefore, travelled in a horizontal plane; (ii) Seshnath Chauhan also had two bullet injuries. The first hit the right eye, rupturing the brain, while the other hit the right chest on the sternal angle, with the bullet being recovered from the back of the chest. These two bullets, too, travelled in a horizontal plane. The evidence of the post-mortem, therefore, clearly establishes that the police were at the same level when they fired at Raj Srivastava and Seshnath Chauhan. This segment of their account is also completely false. **The Commission also notes that though arms and ammunition were allegedly recovered from near the bodies of the deceased, these were not sent for any of the tests that are standard in a thorough police investigation. The Commission has received reports of none of the following tests: (i) on the firearms to**

establish that they were in working order, had been fired recently, and that the cartridges recovered had been or could have been fired from them; (ii) on fingerprints taken from the weapons and matched with those of the two deceased to establish that they had handled them; and (iii) on swabs for gunshot residue taken from their fingers and tested to confirm that they had recently fired weapons. In the absence of any of these tests, there is no proof at all that the two deceased had either handled or fired any weapons. The Commission has examined the record of phone calls made from the telephone number that was allegedly used by Raj Srivastava to extort money. It notes from this, as well as from the copies of the police records that have been sent, that three individuals claimed between the 24th and 25th October that they had received threatening calls from Raj Srivastava. These were Padmakar Verma, Paritosh Ranguta both on the 25th, and Vidyavasini Chaubey on the 24th. However, throughout their testimony, the police have referred primarily to the complaint from Padmakar Verma. This too is strange, since the Commission would have expected the police to have acted as soon as Vidyavasini Chaubey's complaint was lodged on the afternoon of the 24th May, a full day before the other two lodged their FIRs. Even more pertinently, the Commission's officers have established the name of the man to whom the SIM card was registered. It was not Raj Srivastava, but the police have made no efforts to trace this man, to establish if he had any links with him, or if his SIM card had either been stolen or had been given to others. In the absence of any evidence, there is nothing to prove that it was Raj Srivastava who had made the calls to extort money from the three individuals. This claim of the police is therefore also not proven. The Commission has been informed that the two men were criminals, and the nature of their crimes was sufficiently serious for rewards to have been announced for their capture. However, from the documents it has requisitioned, the Commission finds to its surprise that both the rewards were announced on the day the two men were killed. This is far too much of a coincidence. It points to the likelihood that the police tried to build up a case that these men were serious criminals. The rest of their record, also sent by the police, establishes no such thing. For these reasons, the Commission is unable to accept the account given by the police, or its endorsement by the magisterial enquiry. It is clear that the two men were abducted and killed by the police in an extra-judicial execution."

5. The Commission therefore asked the Government of Uttar Pradesh to 'show cause' why it should not recommend relief for the next of kin of Seshnath Chauhan and Raj Srivastava. **The Commission also noted that it had also been told by the families of both the deceased that the dead bodies were not handed over to them. The Commission therefore directed that in its response, the Government of Uttar Pradesh should also establish the claim of the police that they had in fact handed over the bodies to the relatives. If this was not established, it would be a further violation of human rights, in the form of the denial to the next of kin of the consolation of the last rites.**

6. In the instant case, as nothing was heard in the matter the Commission asked the Government of Uttar Pradesh to pay a sum of ₹ 5 lakh each to the next of kins of both the deceased Seshnath Chauhan and Raj Srivastava, which was accepted by the Government of Uttar Pradesh.

5. NHRC Case No 3449/4/23/07-08

1. A complaint was received in the Commission from Smt Anita Devi, in which she alleged that her son Manish Kumar had been abducted by the police on the night of the 4th November 2007, and subsequently killed in a false encounter, together with two others named Mukul Thakur and Subodh Kumar Singh @ Dara Singh. Smt. Anita Devi came to know about the death of her son from the TV report which described the deaths of these three individuals in an alleged police encounter.
2. The Commission noted that the police had stated during the magisterial enquiry that the three men whom they killed had fired 22 rounds at them. Further, the inquest report indicated that 3 pistols and only 4 spent cartridges were recovered from the place of encounter. The Commission observed that there was a substantial difference between the number of spent cartridges recovered, according to the inquest, and the number of rounds that the police claimed had been fired at them. Also, no report of any forensic or ballistics tests was received in the Commission, and "there were no reports that confirmed that fingerprints were taken from the pistol recovered, that these matched the fingerprints of the dead men, that the guns recovered were in working order and had been recently fired, that the cartridges recovered had been fired from these guns, and, finally, that swabs for gunshot residue taken from the fingers of the deceased showed that they had fired weapons". In the absence of this forensic evidence, which would have been standard in any thorough criminal investigation, The Commission noted that there was nothing to establish that these three men had fired the weapons allegedly recovered from the site. The Commission, therefore, asked the SSP Muzaffarpur to

clarify whether these tests were carried out, and if so, to send the reports.

3. These reports were not received by the Commission and the Commission therefore, observed that though the police claimed that they recovered arms and ammunition from the possession of the three men who were killed, the Commission has been sent no proof based on the following standard tests: (i) through tests carried out in a ballistics laboratory that confirmed that the guns were in working order, had been fired recently, and that the cartridges recovered fitted them; (ii) on fingerprints taken from the deceased and matched with those on the guns to establish that they had handled them and; (iii) on swabs for gunshot residue taken from the fingers of the deceased to confirm that they had recently fired weapons.

4. In the absence of any of these reports, the Commission noted that there was nothing to support the police claim that the three men had fired at them, and their claim that they fired in self-defence was also not established. The Commission further observed as under:

   "The post-mortem makes it difficult to accept the account given by the police of how the encounter unfolded. It found the following injuries: (i) Mukesh Thakur had two shots on the chest, lacerating vital organs; (ii) Manish Sharma had three shots to the chest, also lacerating vital organs; (iii) Subodh Kumar Singh had one shot on the chest, one on the neck and two to the back—all shots hit vital organs. The police had fired 15 rounds from 4 pistols. Of these, 9 hit, as established by the postmortem. This is an extraordinary level of accuracy, particularly since the encounter took place late at night on the 5th November, when the meteorological record shows that the moon was in its third quarter, illuminated at 19.9%. Therefore, the encounter took place in almost complete darkness, despite which the police were able to inflict 9 gunshot injuries on three men, who would have taken cover. If this is indeed what the police claim, the records of these four policemen at their annual firing tests should be produced before the Commission to establish that they were sharpshooters. Even more to the point, the nature of the injuries inflicted by pistols cannot be explained if this was a genuine encounter. Since all the bullet wounds caused fatal injuries, the victims would have collapsed as soon as the first shot hit. Not only would the subsequent shots have been unnecessary, even if the police had continued to fire, these would not have hit in the trajectories and on the locations established by the postmortem. Bullet injuries inflicted by shots fired from pistols would have been inflicted in this pattern only if the victims had been surrounded by men who had fired simultaneously at them. This is the pattern of an execution. The evidence before the Commission shows that these three men were victims of an extra-judicial killing."

The Commission therefore asked the Government of Bihar to show cause why it should not recommend relief for the next of kin of Mukul Thakur, Manish Kumar and Subodh Kumar Singh.

5. In response thereto, the Commission was informed that the CB CID has conducted the investigation and the State Government submitted its report to the Commission. The report exonerated the police officials who had participated in the encounter. The report was examined by the Commission and even thereafter certain queries were raised which could not be answered by the CB CID to the

satisfaction of the Commission. The Commission in particular, observed the following:

(i) It appeared that the police opened fire and about 25 empty cases and 9 live rounds were recovered from the spot. However, the ballistic expert had not opined that there was any evidence to indicate that finger prints and hand wash were taken to establish the handling of the weapon by the victims.

(ii) The Police had fired 15 rounds from 4 pistols of which 9 hit the deceased, as established by the post-mortem reports. This indicated extraordinary level of accuracy. Considering the time, which was late at night, the month in which the incident took place and the meteorological record, it was not possible to believe that in view of the darkness, the police could have opened fire on the victims with such accuracy.

(iii) It was indicated that after taking positions the police opened fire, meaning thereby that the police was in a defensive position. Some injuries were on the upper half of the body of the victims. The injuries sustained by all the three persons would have been unlikely if they were in defensive position. It was also indicated that all the injuries were fatal and the persons would have collapsed as soon as the first shot hit them. In a situation like this, subsequent shots would have been unnecessary. However, the police continued to fire. The report submitted by the CB CID did not explain the injury pattern noticed by the Commission as to how they were inflicted on the victims. The Commission observed that the injuries could be inflicted in the pattern indicated only if the victims were surrounded and this was nothing but a pattern of an execution.

(iv) The Commission pointed out that if the criminals fired 20-22 rounds towards the police party the bullets would have hit any other object on the ground, including the police vehicle, but, there was nothing to indicate anywhere in the records that it hit any tree or police jeep, etc. Considering the range of the weapons alleged to have been used having longer firing range, the bullets would have hit some object and should have been photographed and pointed out to the Commission. But, that was not done. The Commission further noted that though called upon to submit the sketch map of the place of occurrence, the same had not been provided. As a matter of fact, such sketch should have been prepared and submitted soon after the incident and a photograph also should have been taken.

(v) In the report of the CB CID the presence of blood at the scene of occurrence had been noted. However, it was indicated that the blood sample could not be taken as the blood was found lying on the metallic road. These made it clear that the injured were on the road and were not taking any shelter of a tree or vehicle or anything. If there was a pool of blood in view of the injury sustained by the three persons, the claim made by the police that the sample could not be lifted could not be accepted. Even earth control sample of the blood had not been taken.

(vi) It was indicated that the SHOs opened fire and the Constables having carbine and rifle did not open fire. There was nothing to indicate that they were asked to open fire. In a situation like this, if it was true, then the other policemen would also have used their weapons to protect the lives of the officers and themselves.

(vii) The Commission noted that "the GD entry does not refer about the weapons or cartridges being taken by the police. Even the entry of weapon used, number of cartridges fired and the number of empty cartridges found are required to be indicated. This is a serious lapse on the part of the police. GD entry, in fact, reflects the immediate action taken by the police before the incident and after the incident."

(viii) More surprisingly, the Commission observed that the statement of the driver of the police jeep indicated that the incident had not taken place in the manner in which it was indicated. The driver had stated that the SHO, Brahmpura on seeing the motor cyclists asked them to stop but they turned back and sped away towards Boria with a view to escape. After that the policemen got down from the jeep and chased the victim. Thereafter he (the driver) heard the sound of firing. The SHO of Brahmpura had however stated that when he tried to stop the motorcyclist the rider started firing on the police, which was a significant contradiction.

6. The Commission observed that under these circumstances, the report submitted by the CB CID also could not be acted upon, and recommended to the Government of Bihar to pay a sum of ₹ 5 lakh each to the next of kins of the 3 deceased. Recommendation of the Commission was accepted by the Government of Bihar.

6. NHRC Case No 522/35/2006-2007

1. The Senior Superintendent of Police, Haridwar sent intimation to the Commission informing that on 12th July 2006 a case crime No 88/06 U/S 364 IPC was registered at Police Station Bhorakalan, district Muzaffarnagar, UP

concerning the incident of kidnapping of a minor child Sandeep @ Sunny aged 14 years. On the night of the 17th July, on receiving information that the kidnappers were moving in Hari Ki Pauri, Haridwar, a substantial police party cordoned off the jungle area of village Missarpur. At about 0058 hours, they spotted two persons on a motorcycle, who on being challenged tried to flee. When asked to surrender, the said motor cycle riders fired on the police and in self-defence police parties also opened fire. After exchange of fire both the motor cycle riders, named and identified as Vipin and Harendra, were found injured. They were taken to hospital where they were declared dead. Arms and ammunition, two country made pistols with jammed cartridges, besides ransom money ₹ 1,48,500 were recovered from them. They were sent to the District Hospital, where they were declared dead. After a search in the area, the kidnapped child was found hiding behind a tree. Concerning the incident of police encounter case crimes Nos 135/06 U/S 307 IPC and 136, 137 of 2006 U/S 25 Arms Act were registered.

2. Regarding the incident a complaint was also received in the Commission alleging death of the two deceased persons Vipin and Harendra in a fake police encounter on 17/18 July 2006 in Haridwar.

3. According to the Inquest and Post-Mortem Reports, both the deceased had died as a result of anti-mortem fire arm injuries. The Magisterial Enquiry Report revealed that on the basis of the testimony of father of the kidnapped boy and police officials involved in the encounter, it revealed that miscreants opened fire on the police party and police party resorted to firing in self-defence.

4. The Commission, however, noted significant discrepancies between the account given by the SSP, Haridwar in his

report to the Commission, and that given to the District Magistrate, Haridwar who conducted the magisterial enquiry. Before the magistrate, the police claimed that they saw a motorcycle with two men who had a child seated between them. This motorcycle was intercepted. The riders tried to escape, but fell down when the motor cycle slipped. The two kidnappers got up and opened fire at the police. The most significant point in this account, the Commission observed, was that the police were aware about the presence of the child and it was difficult to believe that they would have been so irresponsible as to open fire at the kidnappers knowing that the kidnapped child was between them. The Commission also expressed surprise about the account given by the father of the child, who claimed that he handed over ₹ 1.5 lakh to one of the kidnappers, without insisting that his son be produced at the same time. This would have been an elementary precaution to be taken, absence of which created doubts about the nature of the transaction that had been reported. The Commission noted that the magistrate had come to the conclusion that this was a genuine encounter, but the grave discrepancies and serious questions that arose from an examination of these reports made it difficult for the Commission to concur. The Commission also noted that it had received a complaint from the father of Rahul, who had claimed, through a letter sent to the Commission that his son Vipin and his brother Harendra had been picked up by the police and killed in a false encounter. Under these circumstances, the Commission recommended to the Chief Secretary, Uttarakhand, to have a CB CID enquiry conducted into this incident.

5. The Commission examined the CB CID report on this incident and observed the following:

(a) The Commission had noted in its earlier proceedings that it was difficult for it to believe that policeman who had seen the abducted boy with the kidnappers would nevertheless have opened fire, knowing that the hostage might also have been hit. The CB CID enquiry reported that the policemen now claimed that they opened fire only after they had seen, in the light of torches and searchlights that the boy had run away from his kidnappers. However, at no stage the policemen had made this claim earlier. In the first report faxed to the Commission the SSP Haridwar did not claim that the police had even seen the boy with the two kidnappers on their motorcycle. The next report of the SSP Haridwar also did not claim that the police had spotted the boy either on the motorcycle or while the encounter was going on. In the FIR, the policemen recorded that they had seen the boy seated between the two kidnappers, that the men had opened fire, and that they had then returned fire. The implication of this was that the men opened fire while they were on the motorcycle, and the police returned fire while the boy was sandwiched between his kidnappers, and therefore liable to be hit. Perhaps realizing that this would lead to charges that they had endangered the boy's life, the policemen shifted their stand at the magisterial enquiry, claiming that the kidnappers opened fire, and they returned it, only after dismounting from the motorcycle. However, the police did not realize that this too would leave them open to criticism, because, even in this altered account, the boy would have been at risk if the kidnappers had kept him with them when the police opened fire. After the Commission drew this inference they changed their statements again, telling the CB

CID that they had held fire until they had seen the boy run away.

(b) At the magisterial enquiry, the police reported that they put on their torches and searchlights after the firing stopped, not, as they told the CB CID, while it was on. Their first report had the ring of truth, since it was a normal precaution in an exchange of fire in the dark not to give away positions by putting on lights which can be targeted. The CB CID did not question these shifts in the statements, though it was clear that each change was designed to head off the conclusion that flew from their first reports, which is that, if the abducted boy was indeed there, the police opened fire when he was still in the grasp of the kidnappers and therefore likely to be killed.

(c) The CB CID received testimony from the father of Vipin, who had also sent a complaint to the Commission, but rejected it without giving any reasons for doing so. Again, its primary concern seemed to have been not to probe evidence that might go against the police.

(d) The CB CID also did not analyse the evidence of the post-mortem. The locations of the entry and exit wounds showed that the bullets passed through the bodies in a downward plane, which could not be explained from the account given by the police. This trajectory would only be seen if the victims were shot when they were sitting before men who were standing when they fired. This was the scenario of an execution, not of the encounter as reported by the police.

(e) Though arms and ammunition were allegedly recovered from the site, no forensic or ballistics tests were carried out. The CB CID neither asked why this lapse had occurred, not did it have these tests carried out, though these are standard in a professional investigation.

(f) There was nothing to show that fingerprint tests established that the deceased had handled the weapons recovered from the scene; that ballistics tests on the weapons and the ammunition showed that the guns were in working order, had been fired, and that the cartridges recovered had been or could be fired from them; or that swabs for gunshot residue taken from the fingers of the deceased established that they had recently fired guns. There was therefore no independent and scientific evidence to uphold the claim of the police that these men had fired at them.

(g) The policemen gave contradictory testimony even on something as basic as whether the hostage was recovered with one of his hands tied or both. This too the CB CID did not question.

6. For the reasons recorded above, the Commission did not accept the report of the CB CID enquiry which had accepted the account given by the police. The Commission regretted that the CB CID enquiry was perfunctory and unreliable. The Commission also observed that the CB CID, instead of conducting a thorough and impartial enquiry, seemed to have tried to protect the policemen involved in this incident and none of the points that should have been examined in a professional investigation had been considered. The Commission brought this to the attention of the Chief Secretary and the Director General of Police of Uttarakhand for appropriate action.

7. These repeated and grave inconsistencies in the testimony of the police, the continual change in the statements made by them besides the absence of standard scientific tests, made the Commission to draw the conclusion that the

entire account given by the police was concocted. The Commission noted that "it is entirely possible that Vipin and Rahul had abducted a boy, **but it is the circumstances of their deaths that the Commission has to examine,** and, for the reasons given above, it holds that they were executed by the police, not killed in an exchange of fire". **Apart from the circumstances of the encounter, the Commission also noted with grave concern that the father of the deceased of the late Vipin Kumar reiterated to the CB CID enquiry a claim he had made earlier, that the police refused to hand over his son's body, or that of the other man, Rahul, to their families for the last rites. This in itself was a serious violation of the human rights of the family.**

8. The Commission held that the victims were unlawfully killed by police, and in addition to the violation of the right to life of the two men who were killed, there was a further violation of the rights of the next of kin, who were denied the consolation of the last rites, since the bodies were cremated by the police instead of being handed over to the families. For these reasons, the Commission asked the Government of Uttarakhand to pay ₹ 6 lakh to the next of kins of the late Vipin and Rahul. Recommendations made by the Commission were accepted by the Government of Uttarakhand.

7. NHRC Case Number 257/1/2002-2003

1. A complaint was received in the Commission from Human Rights Forum, Gutur alleging killing of one Meda Venkateswarlu on 4th May 2002 by Tedapalli police in Guntur in a fake encounter. Pursuant to the directions, the report received in the Commission from the DIG of Police, Guntur regarding death of Meda Venkateswarlu mentioned that on 4th May 2002, a telephonic call was received at

police station that a man was robbed at the point of revolver at Bund road. The police reached the spot and found a person sitting on the road in suspicious circumstances. On seeing police, he ran away and was chased. The miscreants opened fire on the police party, who retaliated and fired in self-defence, resulting in death of a miscreant, who was subsequently identified to be Meda Venkateswarlu. The inquest on the dead body was conducted by SDM and a case Cr No 109/02 u/s 307 IPC and 25/27 Arms Act was registered at PS Tadepalli, district Guntur. The investigation of the case was being conducted by Madhav Rao, SDPO, Ongole of Prakasam district (another district). It was mentioned that the deceased was a notorious inter-district criminal involved in heinous crimes. He had tendency of attacking the police. In the year 1996, he had attacked one SI of Tedapalli PS for which case Cr No 131/96 u/s 307/32 IPC was registered, which is pending trial vide Session Trial No 544/2001.

2. The Commission examined the detailed report of the magisterial inquest. It noted that Sub-Inspector K Sudhakar had reported to the Magistrate that Meda Venkateswarlu had refused to stop when he had asked him to disclose his identity, and instead had opened fire on the police. The SI had thereafter returned fire with his service revolver. After emptying his revolver, he had reloaded it and continued to fire at Meda Venkateswarlu. Later, after the firing stopped, he had gone up to the body, and recovered various items from it.

3. The Commission observed that it was clear from the testimony of the SI that the encounter took place in almost complete darkness around 3.15 AM. The SI told the Magistrate that after the encounter ended they used the headlight of a scooter to illuminate the spot where the body was lying.

4. The Commission noted that "these being the circumstances of the encounter as explained by the SI, the nature of the injuries found on the body becomes impossible to explain. The autopsy found that the late Meda Venkateswarlu had been shot four times through his chest. All of these had hit vital organs, and each would therefore have been fatal. Shots would have hit in this pattern in a genuine encounter only if they had been fired from a weapon capable of firing a burst. The SI, however, only had a revolver, which he had to reload, which would mean that the first series of shots all missed. It follows that he was then able to inflict four fatal injuries when he resumed firing, still in almost complete darkness. Given the nature of the injuries found in the autopsy, the victim would have collapsed as soon as the first bullet hit. Not only would it have been unnecessary for the other bullets to have been fired thereafter, they could not then have hit in the trajectories established in the post-mortem. The forensic evidence, therefore, establishes that the account of the encounter given by the policemen is false. Instead, it points to the very great likelihood that the SI fired a series of shots into Meda Venkateswarlu when he was unable to defend himself. This evidence establishes a very grievous violation of human rights."
5. The Commission therefore, asked the Government of Andhra Pradesh to 'show cause' why it should not recommend relief for the next of kin of the late Meda Venkateswarlu. The reply received from the Government of Andhra Pradesh mentioned that the deceased had criminal record. The MER was in favour of the police and there was no other option for the police but to open fire at the deceased in self-defence. The Commission observed that all these points were considered by the Commission in the show-cause notice and the State failed to point out infirmity in the

reasons recorded by the Commission except reiterating the earlier version. Also, there was no answer to the queries raised by the Commission. Under the circumstances, the Commission recommended to the Government of Andhra Pradesh to pay a sum of ₹ 5 lakh to the next of kin of deceased Meda Venkateswarlu. Recommendation of the Commission was accepted by the Government of Andhra Pradesh.

Annexure 1

The Protection of Human Rights Act, 1993[1]

[As amended by the Protection of Human Rights (Amendment) Act 2006, No 43 of 2006]

1. Short Title, Extent and Commencement

(1) This Act may be called the Protection of Human Rights Act, 1993.

(2) It extends to the whole of India. Provided that it shall apply to the State of Jammu and Kashmir only in so far as it pertains to the matters relatable to any of the entries enumerated in List I or List III in the Seventh Schedule to the Constitution as applicable to that State.

(3) It shall be deemed to have come into force on the 28th day of September 1993.

2. Definitions

(1) In this Act, unless the context otherwise requires—

(a) 'armed forces' means the naval, military and air forces and includes any other armed forces of the Union;

(b) 'Chairperson' means the Chairperson of the Commission or of the State Commission, as the case may be;

1. Available at the website: http://nhrc.nic.in/documents/Publications/HRActEng.pdf (last visited on 17/09/2014).

(c) 'Commission' means the National Human Rights Commission under section 3;

(d) 'human rights' means the rights relating to life, liberty, equality and dignity of the individual guaranteed by the Constitution or embodied in the International Covenants and enforceable by courts in India.

(e) 'Human Rights Court' means the Human Rights Court specified under section 30;

(f) 'International Covenants' means the International Covenant on Civil and Political Rights and the International Covenant on Economic, Social and Cultural rights adopted by the General Assembly of the United Nations on the 16th December 1996 [and such other covenant or Convention adopted by the General Assembly of the United Nations as the Central Government may, by notification, specify"];

(g) 'Member' means a Member of the Commission or of the State Commission, as the case may be;

(h) 'National Commission for Minorities' means the National Commission for Minorities constituted under section 3 of the National Commission for Minorities Act, 1992;

(i) 'National Commission for the Scheduled Castes' means the National Commission for the Scheduled Castes referred to in Article 338 of the Constitution;

(ia) 'National Commission for the Scheduled Tribes' means the National Commission for the Scheduled Tribes referred to in Article 338A of the Constitution;

(j) 'National Commission for Women' means the National Commission for Women constituted under section 3 of the National Commission for Women Act, 1990;

(k) 'Notification' means a notification published in the official Gazette;

(l) 'Prescribed' means prescribed by rules made under this Act;

(m) 'Public servant' shall have the meaning assigned to it in section 21 of the Indian Penal Code;

(n) 'State Commission' means a State Human Rights Commission constituted under section 21.

(2) Any reference in this Act to a law, which is not in force in the State of Jammu and Kashmir, shall, in relation to that State, be construed as a reference to a corresponding law, if any, in force in that State.

3. Constitution of a National Human Rights Commission

(1) The Central Government shall constitute a body to be known as the National Human Rights Commission to exercise the powers conferred upon, and to perform the functions assigned to it, under this Act.

(2) The Commission shall consist of:

(a) a Chairperson who has been a Chief Justice of the Supreme Court;

(b) one Member who is or has been, a Judge of the Supreme Court;

(c) one Member who is, or has been, the Chief Justice of a High Court;

(d) two Members to be appointed from amongst persons having knowledge of, or practical experience in, matters relating to human rights.

(3) The Chairperson of the National Commission for Minorities, the National Commission for the Scheduled

Castes, the National Commission for the Scheduled Tribes and the National Commission for Women shall be deemed to be Members of the Commission for the discharge of functions specified in clauses (b) to (j) of section 12.

(4) There shall be a Secretary-General who shall be the Chief Executive Officer of the Commission and shall exercise such powers and discharge such functions of the Commission [except judicial functions and the power to make regulations under section 40-B], as may be delegated to him by the Commission or the Chairperson as the case may be.

(5) The headquarters of the Commission shall be at Delhi and the Commission may, with the previous approval of the Central Government, establish offices at other places in India.

4. Appointment of Chairperson and Other Members

(1) The Chairperson and the Members shall be appointed by the President by warrant under his hand and seal; Provided that every appointment under this sub-section shall be made after obtaining the recommendations of a Committee consisting of—

(a) The Prime Minister—Chairperson

(b) Speaker of the House of the People—Member

(c) Minister in-charge of the Ministry of Home Affairs in the Government of India—Member

(d) Leader of the Opposition in the House of the People—Member

(e) Leader of the Opposition in the Council of States—Member

(f) Deputy Chairman of the Council of States—Member

Provided further that no sitting Judge of the Supreme Court or sitting Chief Justice of a High Court shall be appointed except after consultation with the Chief Justice of India.

(2) No appointment of a Chairperson or a Member shall be invalid merely by reason of any vacancy of any member in the Committee referred to in the first proviso to sub-section (1).

5. Resignation and Removal of Chairperson and Members

(1) The Chairperson or any Member may, by notice in writing under his hand addressed to the President of India, resign his office.

(2) Subject to the provisions of sub-section (3), the Chairperson or any Member shall only be removed from his office by order of the President of India on the ground of proved misbehaviour or incapacity after the Supreme Court, on reference being made to it by the President, has, on inquiry held in accordance with the procedure prescribed in that behalf by the Supreme Court, reported that the Chairperson or the Member, as the case may be, ought on any such ground to be removed.

(3) Notwithstanding anything in sub-section (2), the President may, by order, remove from office the Chairperson or any Member if the Chairperson or such Member, as the case may be–

(a) is adjudged an insolvent; or

(b) engages during his term of office in any paid employment outside the duties of his office; or

(c) is unfit to continue in office by reason of infirmity of mind or body; or

(d) is of unsound mind and stands so declared by a competent court; or

(e) is convicted and sentenced to imprisonment for an offence which in the opinion of the President involves moral turpitude.

6. Term of Office of Chairperson and Members

(1) A person appointed as Chairperson shall hold office for a term of five years from the date on which he enters upon his office or until he attains the age of seventy years, whichever is earlier.

(2) A person appointed as a Member shall hold office for a term of five years from the date on which he enters upon his office and shall be eligible for re-appointment for another term of five years. Provided that no Member shall hold office after he has attained the age of seventy years.

(3) On ceasing to hold office, a Chairperson or a Member shall be ineligible for further employment under the Government of India or under the government of any State.

7. Member to Act as Chairperson or to Discharge His Functions in Certain Circumstances

(1) In the event of the occurrence of any vacancy in the office of the Chairperson by reason of his death, resignation or otherwise, the President may, by notification, authorise one of the Members to act as the Chairperson until the appointment of a new Chairperson to fill such vacancy.

(2) When the Chairperson is unable to discharge his functions owing to absence on leave or otherwise, such one of the Members as the President may, by notification, authorise in this behalf, shall discharge the functions of the

Chairperson until the date on which the Chairperson resumes his duties.

8. Terms and Conditions of Service of Chairperson and Members

The salaries and allowances payable to, and other terms and conditions of service of, the [Chairperson and] Members shall be such as may be prescribed. Provided that neither the salary and allowances nor the other terms and conditions of service of the Chairperson or a Member shall be varied to his disadvantage after his appointment.

9. Vacancies, etc, not to Invalidate the Proceedings of the Commission

No act or proceedings of the Commission shall be questioned or shall be invalidated merely on the ground of existence of any vacancy or defect in the constitution of the Commission.

10. Procedure to be Regulated by the Commission

(1) The Commission shall meet at such time and place as the Chairperson may think fit.

(2) Subject to the provisions of this Act and the rules made thereunder, the Commission shall have the power to lay down by regulations its own procedure.

(3) All orders and decisions of the Commission shall be authenticated by the Secretary-General or any other officer of the Commission duly authorised by the Chairperson in this behalf.

11. Officers and Other Staff of the Commission

(1) The Central Government shall make available to the Commission:

(a) an officer of the rank of the Secretary to the Government of India who shall be the Secretary-General of the Commission; and

(b) such police and investigative staff under an officer not below the rank of a Director General of Police and such other officers and staff as may be necessary for the efficient performance of the functions of the Commission.

(2) Subject to such rules as may be made by the Central Government in this behalf, the Commission may appoint such other administrative, technical and scientific staff as it may consider necessary.

(3) The salaries, allowances and conditions of service of the officers and other staff appointed under sub-section (2) shall be such as may be prescribed.

12. Functions of the Commission

The Commission shall perform all or any of the following functions, namely:

(a) inquire, *suo motu* or on a petition presented to it by a victim or any person on his behalf [or on a direction or order of any court], into complaint of

(i) violation of human rights or abetment thereof; or

(ii) negligence in the prevention of such violation, by a public servant;

(b) intervene in any proceeding involving any allegation of violation of human rights pending before a court with the approval of such court;

(c) visit, notwithstanding anything contained in any other law for the time being in force, any jail or other institution under the control of the State Government, where persons are detained or lodged for purposes of treatment, reformation or protection, for the study of the living conditions of the inmates thereof and make recommendations thereon to the government;

(d) review the safeguards provided by or under the Constitution or any law for the time being in force for the protection of human rights and recommend measures for their effective implementation;

(e) review the factors, including acts of terrorism that inhibit the enjoyment of human rights and recommend appropriate remedial measures;

(f) study treaties and other international instruments on human rights and make recommendations for their effective implementation;

(g) undertake and promote research in the field of human rights;

(h) spread human rights literacy among various sections of society and promote awareness of the safeguards available for the protection of these rights through publications, the media, seminars and other available means;

(i) encourage the efforts of non-governmental organisations and institutions working in the field of human rights;

(j) such other functions as it may consider necessary for the protection of human rights.

13. Powers Relating to Inquiries

(1) The Commission shall, while inquiring into complaints under this Act, have all the powers of a civil court trying a suit under the Code of Civil Procedure, 1908, and in particular in respect of the following matters, namely :

(a) summoning and enforcing the attendance of witnesses and examining them on oath;

(b) discovery and production of any document;

(c) receiving evidence on affidavits;

(d) requisitioning any public record or copy thereof from any court or office;

(e) issuing commissions for the examination of witnesses or documents;

(f) any other matter which may be prescribed.

(2) The Commission shall have power to require any person, subject to any privilege which may be claimed by that person under any law for the time being in force, to furnish information on such points or matters as, in the opinion of the Commission, may be useful for, or relevant to, the subject matter of the inquiry and any person so required shall be deemed to be legally bound to furnish such information within the meaning of section 176 and section 177 of the Indian Penal Code.

(3) The Commission or any other officer, not below the rank of a Gazetted Officer, specially authorised in this behalf by the Commission may enter any building or place where the Commission has reason to believe that any document relating to the subject matter of the inquiry may be found, and may seize any such document or take extracts or copies therefrom subject to the provisions of section 100 of the Code of Criminal Procedure, 1973, in so far as it may be applicable.

(4) The Commission shall be deemed to be a civil court and when any offence as is described in section 175, section 178, section 179, section 180 or section 228 of the Indian Penal Code is committed in the view or presence of the Commission, the Commission may, after recording the

facts constituting the offence and the statement of the accused as provided for in the Code of Criminal Procedure, 1973, forward the case to a Magistrate having jurisdiction to try the same and the Magistrate to whom any such case is forwarded shall proceed to hear the complaint against the accused as if the case has been forwarded to him under section 346 of the Code of Criminal Procedure, 1973.

(5) Every proceeding before the Commission shall be deemed to be a judicial proceeding within the meaning of sections 193 and 228, and for the purposes of section 196, of the Indian Penal Code, and the Commission shall be deemed to be a civil court for all the purposes of section 195 and Chapter XXVI of the Code of Criminal Procedure, 1973.

(6) Where the Commission considers it necessary or expedient so to do, it may, by order, transfer any complaint filed or pending before it to the State Commission of the State from which the complaint arises, for disposal in accordance with the provisions of this Act; Provided that no such complaint shall be transferred unless the same is one respecting which the State Commission has jurisdiction to entertain the same.

(7) Every complaint transferred under sub-section (6) shall be dealt with and disposed of by the State Commission as if it were a complaint initially filed before it.

14. Investigation

(1) The Commission may, for the purpose of conducting any investigation pertaining to the inquiry, utilize the services of any officer or investigation agency of the Central Government or any State Government with the concurrence of the Central Government or the State Government, as the case may be.

(2) For the purpose of investigating into any matter pertaining to the inquiry, any officer or agency whose services are utilised under sub-section (1) may, subject to the direction and control of the Commission:

(a) summon and enforce the attendance of any person and examine him;

(b) require the discovery and production of any document; and

(c) requisition any public record or copy thereof from any office.

(3) The provisions of section 15 shall apply in relation to any statement made by a person before any officer or agency whose services are utilised under sub-section (1) as they apply in relation to any statement made by a person in the course of giving evidence before the Commission.

(4) The officer or agency whose services are utilised under sub-section (1) shall investigate into any matter pertaining to the inquiry and submit a report thereon to the Commission within such period as may be specified by the Commission in this behalf.

(5) The Commission shall satisfy itself about the correctness of the facts stated and the conclusion, if any, arrived at in the report submitted to it under sub-section (4) and for this purpose the Commission may make such inquiry (including the examination of the person or persons who conducted or assisted in the investigation) as it thinks fit.

15. Statement Made by Persons to the Commission

No statement made by a person in the course of giving evidence before the Commission shall subject him to, or be used against him in, any civil or criminal proceeding except a prosecution for giving false evidence by such statement: Provided that the statement—

(a) is made in reply to the question which he is required by the Commission to answer; or

(b) is relevant to the subject matter of the inquiry.

16. Persons Likely to be Prejudicially Affected to be Heard

If, at any stage of the inquiry, the Commission:

(a) considers it necessary to inquire into the conduct of any person; or

(b) is of the opinion that the reputation of any person is likely to be prejudicially affected by the inquiry;

it shall give to that person a reasonable opportunity of being heard in the inquiry and to produce evidence in his defence. Provided that nothing in this section shall apply where the credit of a witness is being impeached.

17. Inquiry into Complaints

The Commission while inquiring into the complaints of violations of human rights may—

(i) call for information or report from the Central Government or any State Government or any other authority or organization subordinate thereto within such time as may be specified by it:

Provided that—

(a) if the information or report is not received within the time stipulated by the Commission, it may proceed to inquire into the complaint on its own;

(b) if, on receipt of information or report, the Commission is satisfied either that no further inquiry is required or that the required action has been initiated or taken by the concerned government or authority, it may not proceed with the complaint and inform the complainant accordingly;

(ii) without prejudice to anything contained in clause (i), if it considers necessary, having regard to the nature of the complaint, initiate an inquiry.

18. Steps During and After Inquiry

The Commission may take any of the following steps during or upon the completion of an inquiry held under this Act, namely—

(a) where the inquiry discloses the commission of violation of human rights or negligence in the prevention of violation of human rights or abetment thereof by a public servant, it may recommend to the concerned government or authority—

   (i) to make payment of compensation or damages to the complainant or to the victim or the members of his family as the Commission may consider necessary;

   (ii) to initiate proceedings for prosecution or such other suitable action as the Commission may deem fit against the concerned person or persons;

   (iii) to take such further action as it may think fit;

(b) approach the Supreme Court or the High Court concerned for such directions, orders or writs as that court may deem necessary;

(c) recommend to the concerned government or authority at any stage of the inquiry for the grant of such immediate interim relief to the victim or the members of his family as the Commission may consider necessary;

(d) subject to the provisions of clause (e), provide a copy of the inquiry report to the petitioner or his representative;

(e) the Commission shall send a copy of its inquiry report together with its recommendations to the concerned government or authority and the concerned government or authority shall, within a period of one month, or such further time as the Commission may allow, forward its comments on the report, including the action taken or proposed to be taken thereon, to the Commission;

(f) the Commission shall publish its inquiry report together with the comments of the concerned government or authority, if any, and the action taken or proposed to be taken by the concerned government or authority on the recommendations of the Commission.

19. Procedure with Respect to Armed Forces

(1) Notwithstanding anything contained in this Act, while dealing with complaints of violation of human rights by members of the armed forces, the Commission shall adopt the following procedure, namely:-

(a) it may, either on its own motion or on receipt of a petition, seek a report from the Central Government;

(b) after the receipt of the report, it may, either not proceed with the complaint or, as the case may be, make its recommendations to that government.

(2) The Central Government shall inform the Commission of the action taken on the recommendations within three months or such further time as the Commission may allow.

(3) The Commission shall publish its report together with its recommendations made to the Central Government and the action taken by that government on such recommendations.

(4) The Commission shall provide a copy of the report published under sub-section (3) to the petitioner or his representative.

20. Annual and Special Reports of the Commission

(1) The Commission shall submit an annual report to the Central Government and to the State Government concerned and may at any time submit special reports on any matter which, in its opinion, is of such urgency or importance that it should not be deferred till submission of the annual report.

(2) The Central Government and the State Government, as the case may be, shall cause the annual and special reports of the Commission to be laid before each House of Parliament or the State Legislature respectively, as the case may be, along with a memorandum of action taken or proposed to be taken on the recommendations of the Commission and the reasons for non-acceptance of the recommendations, if any.

21. Constitution of State Human Rights Commissions

(1) A State Government may constitute a body to be known as the ... (name of the State) Human Rights Commission to exercise the powers conferred upon, and to perform the functions assigned to, a State Commission under this chapter.

(2) [The State Commission shall, with effect from such date as the State Government may by notification specify, consist of—

(a) a Chairperson who has been a Chief Justice of a High Court;

(b) one Member who is, or has been, a Judge of a High Court or District Judge in the State with a minimum of seven years' experience as District Judge;

(c) one Member to be appointed from amongst persons having knowledge of, or practical experience in, matters relating to human rights.]

(3) There shall be a Secretary who shall be the Chief Executive Officer of the State Commission and shall exercise such powers and discharge such functions of the State Commission as it may delegate to him.

(4) The headquarters of the State Commission shall be at such place as the State Government may, by notification, specify.

(5) A State Commission may inquire into violation of human rights only in respect of matters relatable to any of the entries enumerated in List II and List III in the Seventh Schedule to the Constitution:

Provided that if any such matter is already being inquired into by the Commission or any other Commission duly constituted under any law for the time being in force, the State Commission shall not inquire into the said matter:

Provided further that in relation to the Jammu and Kashmir Human Rights Commission, this sub-section shall have effect as if for the words and figures "List II and List III in the Seventh Schedule to the Constitution", the words and figures "List III in the Seventh Schedule to the Constitution as applicable to the State of Jammu and Kashmir and in respect of matters in relation to which the Legislature of that State has power to make laws" had been substituted.

(6) [Two or more State Governments may, with the consent of a Chairperson or Member of a State Commission, appoint such Chairperson or, as the case may be, such Member of another State Commission simultaneously if such Chairperson or Member consents to such appointment:

Provided that every appointment made under this sub-section shall be made after obtaining the recommendations of the Committee referred to in sub-section (1) of section 22 in respect of the State for which a common Chairperson or Member, or both, as the case may be, is to be appointed].

22. Appointment of Chairperson and Members of State Commission

(1) The Chairperson and [Members] shall be appointed by the Governor by warrant under his hand and seal: Provided that every appointment under this sub-section shall be made after obtaining the recommendation of a Committee consisting of

(a) the Chief Minister—Chairperson

(b) Speaker of the Legislative Assembly—Member

(c) Minister in-charge of the Department of Home, in that State—Member

(d) Leader of the Opposition in the Legislative Assembly—Member

Provided further that where there is a Legislative Council in a State, the Chairman of that Council and the Leader of the Opposition in that Council shall also be members of the Committee.

Provided also that no sitting Judge of a High Court or a sitting District Judge shall be appointed except after consultation with the Chief Justice of the High Court of the concerned State.

(2) No appointment of a Chairperson or a Member of the State Commission shall be invalid merely by reason of [any vacancy of any Member in the Committee referred to in sub-section (1).

23. Resignation and Removal of Chairperson or a Member of the State Commission

(1) The Chairperson or a Member of a State Commission may, by notice in writing under his hand addressed to the Governor, resign his office.

(1A) Subject to the provisions of sub-section (2), the Chairperson or any Member of the State Commission shall only be removed from his office by order of the President on the ground of proved misbehaviour or incapacity after the Supreme Court, on a reference being made to it by the President, has, on inquiry held in accordance with the procedure prescribed in that behalf by the Supreme Court, reported that the Chairperson or such Member, as the case may be, ought on any such ground to be removed.]

(2) Notwithstanding anything in sub-section (1A), the President may by order remove from office the Chairperson or any [Member] if the Chairperson or such [Member], as the case may be—

(a) is adjudged an insolvent; or

(b) engages during his term of office in any paid employment outside the duties of his office; or

(c) is unfit to continue in office by reason of infirmity of mind or body; or

(d) is of unsound mind and stands so declared by a competent court; or

(e) is convicted and sentenced to imprisonment for an offence which in the opinion of the President involves moral turpitude.

24. Term of Office of Chairperson and Members of the State Commission

(1) A person appointed as Chairperson shall hold office for a term of five years from the date on which he enters upon his office or until he attains the age of seventy years, whichever is earlier;

(2) A person appointed as a Member shall hold office for a term of five years from the date on which he enters upon his office and shall be eligible for re-appointment for another term of five years;

Provided that no Member shall hold office after he has attained the age of seventy years.

(3) On ceasing to hold office, a Chairperson or a Member shall be ineligible for further employment under the Government of a State or under the Government of India.

25. Member to Act as Chairperson or to Discharge His Functions in Certain Circumstances

(1) In the event of the occurrence of any vacancy in the office of the Chairperson by reason of his death, resignation or otherwise, the Governor may, by notification, authorize one of the Members to act as the Chairperson until the appointment of a new Chairperson to fill such vacancy.

(2) When the Chairperson is unable to discharge his functions owing to absence on leave or otherwise, such one of the Members as the Governor may, by notification, authorize in this behalf, shall discharge the functions of the Chairperson until the date on which the Chairperson resumes his duties.

26. Terms and Conditions of Service of Chairperson and Members of the State Commissions

The salaries and allowances payable to, and other terms and conditions of service of, the Chairperson and Members shall be such as may be prescribed by the State Government; Provided that neither the salary and allowances nor the other terms and conditions of service of the Chairperson or a Member shall be varied to his disadvantage after his appointment.

27. Officers and Other Staff of the State Commission

(1) The State Government shall make available to the Commission

(a) an officer not below the rank of a Secretary to the State Government who shall be the Secretary of the State Commission; and

(b) such police and investigative staff under an officer not below the rank of an Inspector General of Police and such other officers and staff as may be necessary for the efficient performance of the functions of the State Commission.

(2) Subject to such rules as may be made by the State Government in this behalf, the State Commission may appoint such other administrative, technical and scientific staff as it may consider necessary.

(3) The salaries, allowances and conditions of service of the officers and other staff appointed under sub-section (2) shall be such as may be prescribed by the State Government.

28. Annual and Special Reports of State Commission

(1) The State Commission shall submit an annual report to the State Government and may at any time submit special

reports on any matter which, in its opinion, is of such urgency or importance that it should not be deferred till submission of the annual report.

(2) The State Government shall cause the annual and special reports of the State Commission to be laid before each House of State Legislature where it consists of two Houses, or where such Legislature consists of one House, before that House along with a memorandum of action taken or proposed to be taken on the recommendations of the State Commission and the reasons for non-acceptance of the recommendations, if any.

29. Application of Certain Provisions Relating to National Human Rights Commission to State Commissions

The provisions of sections 9, 10, 12, 13, 14, 15, 16, 17 and 18 shall apply to a State Commission and shall have effect, subject to the following modifications, namely—

(a) references to 'Commission' shall be construed as references to 'State Commission';

(b) in section 10, in sub-section (3), for the word 'Secretary General', the word 'Secretary' shall be substituted;

(c) in section 12, clause (f) shall be omitted;

(d) in section 17, in clause (i), the words 'Central Government or any' shall be omitted,

36. Matters not Subject to Jurisdiction of the Commission

(1) The Commission shall not inquire into any matter which is pending before a State Commission or any other Commission duly constituted under any law for the time being in force.

(2) The Commission or the State Commission shall not inquire into any matter after the expiry of one year from

the date on which the act constituting violation of human rights is alleged to have been committed.

37. Constitution of Special Investigation Teams

Notwithstanding anything contained in any other law for the time being in force, where the government considers it necessary so to do, it may constitute one or more special investigation teams, consisting of such police officers as it thinks necessary for purposes of investigation and prosecution of offences arising out of violations of human rights.

Annexure 2

NHRC's Guidelines/Procedures to be Followed in Cases of Deaths Caused in Policy Action[1]

(i) When the police officer in charge of a Police Station receives information about death in an encounter with the police, he shall enter that information in the appropriate register.

(ii) Where the police officers belonging to the same Police Station are members of the encounter party, whose action resulted in death, it is desirable that such cases are made over for investigation to some other independent investigating agency, such as State CB CID.

(iii) Whenever a specific complaint is made against the police alleging commission of a criminal act on their part, which makes out a cognizable case of culpable homicide, an FIR to this effect must be registered under appropriate sections of the IPC. Such case shall be investigated by State CB CID or any other specialized investigation agency.

(iv) A magisterial enquiry must be held in all cases of death which occurs in the course of police action, as expeditiously as possible, preferably, within three months. The relatives of the deceased, eye witness, witnesses having information

1. Available at the website: http://nhrc.nic.in/documents/Death%20During%20the%20course%20of%20Police%20Action.pdf (last visited on 17/09/2014).

of the circumstances leading to encounter, police station records, etc must be examined while conducting such enquiry.

(v) Prompt prosecution and disciplinary action must be initiated against all delinquent officers found guilty in the magisterial enquiry/police investigation.

(vi) No out-of-turn promotion or instant gallantry regards shall be bestowed on the concerned officers soon after the occurrence. It must be ensured at all costs that such rewards are given/commended only when the gallantry of the concerned officer is established beyond doubt.

(vii) All cases of deaths in police action in the states shall be reported to the Commission by the Senior Superintendent of Police/Superintendent of Police of the District within 48 hours of such death in the following format—

1. Date and place of occurrence
2. Police station, district
3. Circumstances leading to death:
   (i) Self defence in encounter
   (ii) In course of dispersal of unlawful assembly
   (iii) In the course of effecting arrest
   (iv) Any other circumstances
4. Brief facts of the incident
5. Criminal case number
6. Investigating agency

(b) A second report must be sent in all cases of death in police action in the state by the Senior Superintendent of Police/Superintendent of Police to the Commission within three months providing following information:

1. Post-mortem report
2. Inquest report
3. Findings of the magisterial enquiry/enquiry by senior officers disclosing:
   (i) Name and designation of police official, if found responsible for the death;
   (ii) Whether use of force was justified and action taken was lawful;
   (iii) Result of the forensic examination of 'hand wash' of the deceased to ascertain the presence of residue of gun powder to justify exercise of right of self defence; and
   (iv) Report of the Ballistic Expert on examination of the weapons alleged to have been used by the deceased and his companions.

Annexure 3

Provisions Contained in the Indian Penal Code, 1860 and the Criminal Procedure Code, 1973 Relevant to Situations Involving Use of Force by Police

(A) Provisions Contained in the Indian Penal Code, 1860 Related to the Right of Private Defence of the Body and of Property

Section 97. Right of Private Defence of the Body and of Property—Every person has a right, subject to the restrictions contained in section 99, to defend—

First—His own body and the body of any other person, against any offence affecting the human body;

Secondly—The property, whether movable or immovable, of himself or of any other person, against any act which is an offence falling under the definition of theft, robbery, mischief or criminal trespass, or which is an attempt to commit theft, robbery, mischief or criminal trespass.

Section 99. Act against which there is no Right of Private Defence—There is no Right of Private Defence against an act which does not reasonably cause the apprehension of death or of grievous hurt, if done, or attempted to be done, by a public servant acting in good faith under colour of his office, though that act, may not be strictly justifiable by law.

There is no Right of Private Defence against an act which does not reasonably cause the apprehension of death or of grievous hurt, if done, or attempted to be done, by the direction of a public servant acting in good faith under colour of his office, though that direction may not be strictly justifiable by law.

There is no Right of Private Defence in cases in which there is time to have recourse to the protection of the public authorities.

Extent to which the right may be exercised—The right to private defence in no case extends to the inflicting of more harm than it is necessary to inflict for the purpose of defence.

Explanation 1: A person is not deprived of the Right of Private Defence against an act done, or attempted to be done, by a public servant, as such, unless he knows or has reason to believe, that the person doing the act is such public servant.

Explanation 2: A person is not deprived of the Right of Private Defence against an act done, or attempted to be done, by the direction of a public servant, unless he knows, or has reason to believe, that the person doing the act is acting by such direction, or unless such person states the authority under which he acts, or if he has authority in writing, unless he produces such authority, if demanded.

Section 100. When the Right of Private Defence of the Body extends to causing death—The Right of Private Defence of the Body extends, under the restrictions mentioned in the last preceding section, to the voluntary causing of death or of any other harm to the assailant, if the offence which occasions the exercise of the right be of any of the descriptions hereinafter enumerated, namely—

First—Such an assault as may reasonably cause the apprehension that death will otherwise be the consequence of such assault;

Secondly—Such an assault as may reasonably cause the apprehension that grievous hurt will otherwise be the consequence of such assault;

Thirdly—An assault with the intention of committing rape;

Fourthly—An assault with the intention of gratifying unnatural lust;

Fifthly—An assault with the intention of kidnapping or abducting;

Sixthly—An assault with the intention of wrongfully confining a person, under circumstances which may reasonably cause him to apprehend that he will be unable to have recourse to the public authorities for his release.

Section 101. When such right extends to causing any harm other than death—If the offence be not of any of the descriptions enumerated in the last preceding section, the Right of Private Defence of the Body does not extend to the voluntary causing of death to the assailant, but does extend, under the restrictions mentioned in section 99, to the voluntary causing to the assailant of any harm other than death.

Section 102. Commencement and continuance of the Right of Private Defence of the Body—The Right of Private Defence of the Body commences as soon as a reasonable apprehension of danger to the body arises from an attempt or threat to commit the offence though the offence may not have been committed; and it continues as long as such apprehension of danger to the body continues.

Section 103. When the Right of Private Defence of Property extends to causing death—The Right of Private Defence of

Property extends, under the restrictions mentioned in section 99, to the voluntary causing of death or of any other harm to the wrong-doer, if the offence, the committing of which, or the attempting to commit which, occasions the exercise of the right, be an offence of any of the descriptions hereinafter enumerated, namely:

First—Robbery;

Secondly—House-breaking by night;

Thirdly—Mischief by fire committed on any building, tent or vessel, which building, tent or vessel is used as a human dwelling, or as a place for the custody of property;

Fourthly—Theft, mischief, or house-trespass, under such circumstances as may reasonably cause apprehension that death or grievous hurt will be the consequence, if such Right of Private Defence is not exercised.

Section 104. When such right extends to causing any harm other than death—If the offence, the committing of which, or the attempting to commit which occasions the exercise of the Right of Private Defence, be theft, mischief, or criminal trespass, not of any of the descriptions enumerated in the last preceding section, that right does not extend to the voluntary causing of death, but does extend, subject to the restrictions mentioned in section 99, to the voluntary causing to the wrong-doer of any harm other than death.

Section 105. Commencement and continuance of the Right of Private Defence of Property—The Right of Private Defence of Property commences when a reasonable apprehension of danger to the property commences.

The Right of Private Defence of Property against theft continues till the offender has effected his retreat with the property or either the assistance of the public authorities is obtained, or the property has been recovered.

The Right of Private Defence of Property against robbery continues as long as the offender causes or attempts to cause to any person death or hurt or wrongful restraint or as long as the fear of instant death or of instant hurt or of instant personal restraint continues.

The Right of Private Defence of Property against criminal trespass or mischief continues as long as the offender continues in the commission of criminal trespass or mischief.

The Right of Private Defence of Property against house-breaking by night continues as long as the house-trespass which has been begun by such house-breaking continues.

Section 106. Right of Private Defence against deadly assault when there is risk of harm to innocent person—If in the exercise of the Right of Private Defence against an assault which reasonably causes the apprehension of death, the defender be so situated that he cannot effectually exercise that right without risk of harm to an innocent person his Right of Private Defence extends to the running of that risk.

Illustration: A is attacked by a mob who attempt to murder him. He cannot effectually exercise his Right of Private Defence without firing on the mob, and he cannot fire without risk of harming young children who are mingled with the mob. A commits no offence if by so firing he harms any of the children.

(B) Provisions Contained in the Indian Penal Code, 1860 Related to the Homicide

Section 299. Culpable homicide—Whoever causes death by doing an act with the intention of causing death, or with the intention of causing such bodily injury as is likely to cause death, or with the knowledge that he is likely by such act to cause death, commits the offence of culpable homicide.

Section 300. Murder—Except in the cases hereinafter excepted, culpable homicide is murder, if the act by which the death is caused is done with the intention of causing death; or—

Secondly—If it is done with the intention of causing such bodily injury as the offender knows to be likely to cause the death of the person to whom the harm is caused; or

Thirdly—If it is done with the intention of causing bodily injury to any person and the bodily injury intended to be inflicted is sufficient in the ordinary course of nature to cause death; or

Fourthly—If the person committing the act knows that it is so imminently dangerous that it must, in all probability, cause death or such bodily injury as is likely to cause death, and commits such act without any excuse for incurring the risk of causing death or such injury as aforesaid.

Exception 1: When culpable homicide is not murder—Culpable homicide is not murder if the offender, whilst deprived of the power of self-control by grave and sudden provocation, causes the death of the person who gave the provocation or causes the death of any other person by mistake or accident.

The above exception is subject to the following provisos—

First—That the provocation is not sought or voluntarily provoked by the offender as an excuse for killing or doing harm to any person.

Secondly—That the provocation is not given by anything done in obedience to the law, or by a public servant in the lawful exercise of the powers of such public servant.

Thirdly—That the provocation is not given by anything done in the lawful exercise of the Right of Private Defence.

Explanation: Whether the provocation was grave and sudden enough to prevent the offence from amounting to murder is a question of fact.

Exception 2: Culpable homicide is not murder if the offender in the exercise in good faith of the Right of Private Defence of Person or Property, exceeds the power given to him by law and causes the death of the person against whom he is exercising such right of defence without premeditation, and without any intention of doing more harm than is necessary for the purpose of such defence.

Exception 3: Culpable homicide is not murder if the offender, being a public servant or aiding a public servant acting for the advancement of public justice, exceeds the powers given to him by law, and causes death by doing an act which he, in good faith, believes to be lawful and necessary for the due discharge of his duty as such public servant and without ill-will towards the person whose death is caused.

Exception 4: Culpable homicide is not murder if it is committed without premeditation in a sudden fight in the heat of passion upon a sudden quarrel and without the offender having taken undue advantage or acted in a cruel or unusual manner.

Exception 5: Culpable homicide is not murder when the person whose death is caused, being above the age of eighteen years, suffers death or takes the risk of death with his own consent.

Section 301. Culpable homicide by causing death of person other than person whose death was intended—If a person, by doing anything which he intends or knows to be likely to cause death, commits culpable homicide by causing the death of any person, whose death he neither intends nor knows himself to be likely to cause, the culpable homicide committed by the offender is of the description of which it would have been if he had caused the death of the person whose death he intended or knew himself to be likely to cause.

Section 302. Punishment for murder—Whoever commits murder shall be punished with death, or imprisonment for life and shall also be liable to fine.

Section 304. Punishment for culpable homicide not amounting to murder—Whoever commits culpable homicide not amounting to murder shall be punished with imprisonment for life, or imprisonment of either description for a term which may extend to ten years, and shall also be liable to fine, if the act by which the death is caused is done with the intention of causing death, or of causing such bodily injury as is likely to cause death; or with imprisonment of either description for a term which may extend to ten years, or with fine, or with both, if the act is done with the knowledge that it is likely to cause death, but without any intention to cause death, or to cause such bodily injury as is likely to cause death,

Section 304A. Causing death by negligence—Whoever causes the death of any person by doing any rash or negligent act not amounting to culpable homicide, shall be punished with imprisonment of either description for a term which may extend to two years, or with fine, or with both.

(C) Provisions Contained in the Criminal Procedure Code, 1973 Related to the Use of Force during Arrest of an Offender

Section 46. Arrest how made—

(1) In making an arrest the police officer or other person making the same shall actually touch or confine the

body of the person to be arrested, unless there be a submission to the custody by word or action.

(2) If such person forcibly resists the endeavour to arrest him, or attempts to evade the arrest, such police officer or other person may use all means necessary to effect the arrest.

(3) Nothing in this section gives a right to cause the death of a person who is not accused of an offence punishable with death or with imprisonment for life.

(D) Provisions Contained in the Indian Evidence Act, 1872 Related to the Plea of Exercise of Right of Private Defence

Section 105. Burden of proving that case of accused comes within exceptions—When a person is accused of any offence, the burden of proving the existence of circumstances bringing the case within any of the General Exceptions in the Indian Penal Code (45 of 1860), or within any special exception or proviso contained in any other part of the same Code, or in any law defining the offence, is upon him, and the court shall presume the absence of such circumstances.

Annexure 4

The Armed Forces (Jammu and Kashmir Special Powers Act, 1990)

Number 21 of 1990 [10th September 1990][1]

An Act to enable certain special powers to be conferred upon members of the armed forces in the disturbed areas in the State of Jammu and Kashmir.

BE it enacted by Parliament in the Forty-first Year of the Republic of India as follows:

1. Short Title, Extent and Commencement

(1) This Act may be called the Armed Forces (Jammu and Kashmir) Special Powers Act, 1990.

(2) It extends to the whole of the State of Jammu and Kashmir.

(3) It shall be deemed to have come into force on the 5th day of July 1990.

2. Definitions

In this Act, unless the context otherwise requires,—

(a) 'armed forces' means the military forces and the air forces operating as land forces and includes any other armed forces of the Union so operating

---

1. Available at the website: http://mha.nic.in/sites/upload_files/mha/files/pdf/Armedforces%20_J&K_%20Splpowersact1990.pdf (last visited on 17/09/2014).

(b) 'disturbed area' means an area which is for the time being declared by notification under section 3 to be a disturbed area;

(c) all other words and expressions used herein, but not defined and defined in the Air Force Act 1950, or the Army Act, 1950 shall have the meanings respectively assigned to them in those Acts.

3. Powers to Declare Areas to be Disturbed Areas

If, in relation to the State of Jammu and Kashmir, the Governor of that State or the Central Government, is of opinion that the whole or any part of the State is in such a disturbed and dangerous condition that the use of armed forces in aid of the civil power is necessary to prevent—

(a) activities involving terrorist acts directed towards overawing the government as by law established or striking terror in the people or any section of the people or alienating any section of the people or adversely affecting the harmony amongst different sections of the people;

(b) activities directed towards disclaiming, questioning or disrupting the sovereignty and territorial integrity of India or bringing about cession of a part of the territory of India or secession of a part of the territory of India from the Union or causing insult to the Indian National Flag, the Indian National Anthem and the Constitution of India, the Governor of the State or the Central Government, may, by notification in the Official Gazette, declare the whole or any part of the State to be a disturbed area.

Explanation: In this section, 'terrorist act' has the same meaning as in Explanation to article 248 of the

Constitution of India as applicable to the State of Jammu and Kashmir.

4. Special Powers of the Armed Forces

Any commissioned officer, warrant officer, non-commissioned officer or any other person of equivalent rank in the armed forces may, in a disturbed area,—

(a) if he is of opinion that it is necessary so to do for the maintenance of public order, after giving such due warning as he may consider necessary, fire upon or otherwise use force, even to the causing of death, against any person who is acting in contravention of any law or order for the time being in force in the disturbed area prohibiting the assembly of five or more persons or the carrying of weapons or of things capable of being used as weapons or of firearms, ammunition or explosive substances;

(b) if he is of opinion that it is necessary so to do, destroy any arms dump, prepared or fortified position or shelter from which armed attacks are made or are likely to be made or are attempted to be made, or any structure used as training camp for armed volunteers or utilized as a hide-out by armed gangs or absconders wanted for any offence;

(c) arrest, without warrant, any person who has committed a cognizable offence or against whom a reasonable suspicion exists that he has committed or is about to commit a cognizable offence and may use such force as may be necessary to effect the arrest;

(d) enter and search, without warrant, any premises to make any such arrest as aforesaid or to recover any person believed to be wrongfully restrained or confined or any property reasonably suspected to be stolen property or any arms, ammunition or explosive substances believed to be unlawfully kept in such premises, and may for that purpose use such force as may be necessary, and seize any such property, arms, ammunition or explosive substances;

(e) stop, search and seize any vehicle or vessel reasonably suspected to be carrying any person who is a proclaimed offender, or any person who has committed a non-cognizable offence, or against whom a reasonable suspicion exists that he has committed or is about to commit a non-cognizable offence, or any person who is carrying any arms, ammunition or explosive substance believed to be unlawfully held by him, and may, for that purpose, use such force as may be necessary to effect such stoppage, search or seizure, as the case may be.

5. Power of Search to Include Powers to Break Open Locks, etc

Every person making a search under this Act shall have the power to break open the lock of any door, almirah, safe, box, cupboard, drawer, package or other thing, if the key thereof is withheld.

6. Arrested Persons and Seized Property to be Made Over to the Police

Any person arrested and taken into custody under this Act and every property, arms, ammunition or explosive substance or any vehicle or vessel seized under this Act, shall be made over to the officer-in-charge of the nearest police station with the least possible delay, together with a report of the circumstances occasioning the arrest, or as the case may be, occasioning the seizure of such property, arms, ammunition or explosive substance or any vehicle or vessel, as the case may be.

7. Protection of Persons Acting in Good Faith under this Act

No prosecution, suit or other legal proceeding shall be instituted, except with the previous sanction of the Central Government, against any person in respect of anything done or purported to be done in exercise of the powers conferred by this Act.

Annexure 5

The Jammu and Kashmir Disturbed Areas Act, 1992[1]

1. Enacted by the President in the Forty-third Year of the Republic of India An Act to provide for better provision for the suppression of disorder and for the restoration and maintenance of public order in disturbed areas in Jammu and Kashmir In exercise of the powers conferred by Section 3 of the Jammu and Kashmir State Legislature (Delegation of Powers) Act, 1992 (21 of 1992), the President is pleased to enact as follows:

2. Definition

(1) In this Act, 'disturbed area' means an area which is for the time being declared by notification under section 3—to be a disturbed area.

(2) All other words and expressions used herein and not defined, but defined in any other law for the time being in force in the State of Jammu and Kashmir, shall have the meanings respectively assigned to them in such law.

3. Powers to Declare Areas to be Disturbed Areas

The State Government may, by notification in the Official Gazette, declare that the whole or any part of any district of

---

1. Available at the website: http://acts.gov.in/JK/2154.pdf (last visited on 17/09/2014).

Jammu and Kashmir as may be specified in the notification, in a disturbed area.

4. Power to Fire upon Persons Contravening Certain Orders

In a 'disturbed area', any Magistrate or Police Officer not below the rank of Sub-Inspector or Head Constable in case of the Armed Branch of the Police may, if he is of opinion that it is necessary so to do for the maintenance of public order, after giving such due warning, as he may consider necessary, fire upon, or otherwise use force, even to the causing of death, against any person who is indulging in any act which may result in serious breach of public order or is acting in contravention of any law or order for the time being in force, prohibiting the assembly of five or more persons or the carrying of weapons or of things capable of being used as weapons or of firearms, ammunition or explosive substances.

5. Powers to Destroy Arms Dump, Fortified Positions, etc

In a 'disturbed area', any Magistrate or Police Officer not below the rank of a Sub-Inspector may, if he is of the opinion that it is necessary so to do, destroy any arms dump, prepared or fortified position of shelter from which aimed attacks are made or are likely to be made or are attempted to be made or any structure used as a training camp for armed volunteers or utilised as a hideout by armed gangs or absconders wanted for any offence.

6. Protection of Persons Acting under Sections 4 and 5

No suit, prosecution, or other legal proceedings shall be instituted except with the previous sanction of the State Government against any person in respect of anything done or purporting to be done in exercise of the powers conferred by Sections 4 and 5.

Annexure 6

Code of Conduct for the Police in India[1]

The guidelines for the code of conduct for the police were issued by the Ministry of Home Affairs and communicated to Chief Secretaries of all States/Union Territories and Heads of Central Police Organizations on July 4, 1985.

1. The police must bear faithful allegiance to the Constitution of India and respect and uphold the rights of the citizens as guaranteed by it.
2. The police should not question the propriety or necessity of any law duly enacted. They should enforce the law firmly and impartially, without fear or favour, malice or vindictiveness.
3. The police should recognize and respect the limitations of their powers and functions. They should not usurp or even seem to usurp the functions of the judiciary and sit in judgment on cases to avenge individuals and punish the guilty.
4. In securing the observance of law or in maintaining order, the police should as far as practicable, use the methods of persuasion, advice and warning. When the application of force becomes inevitable, only the irreducible minimum of force required in the circumstances should be used.
5. The prime duty of the police is to prevent crime and

---

1. Available at the website: http://police.pondicherry.gov.in/MHA%20-%20Model%20Code%20of%20Conduct%20-%20Indian%20Police.pdf (last visited on 17/09/2014).

disorder and the police must recognize that the test of their efficiency is the absence of both and not the visible evidence of police action in dealing with them.

6. The police must recognize that they are members of the public, with the only difference that in the interest of the society and on its behalf they are employed to give full time attention to duties, which are normally incumbent on every citizen to perform.
7. The police should realize that the efficient performance of their duties would be dependent on the extent of ready cooperation that they receive from the public. This, in turn, will depend on their ability to secure public approval of their conduct and actions and to earn and retain public respect and confidence.
8. The police should always keep the welfare of the people in mind and be sympathetic and considerate towards them. They should always be ready to offer individual service and friendship and render necessary assistance to all without regard to their wealth and/or social standing.
9. The police should always place duty before self, should maintain calm in the face of danger, scorn or ridicule and should be ready to sacrifice their lives in protecting those of others.
10. The police should always be courteous and well mannered; they should be dependable and impartial; they should possess dignity and courage; and should cultivate character and the trust of the people.
11. Integrity of the highest order is the fundamental basis of the prestige of the police. Recognizing this, the police must keep their private lives scrupulously clean, develop self-restraint and be truthful and honest in thought and deed, in both personal and official life, so that the public may regard them as exemplary citizens.

12. The police should recognize that their full utility to the State is best ensured only by maintaining a high standard of discipline, faithful performance of duties in accordance with law and implicit obedience to the lawful directions of commanding ranks and absolute loyalty to the force and by keeping themselves in the state of constant training and preparedness.
13. As members of a secular, democratic state, the police should strive continually to rise above personal prejudices and promote harmony and the spirit of common brotherhood amongst all the people of India, transcending religious, linguistic or sectional diversities and to renounce practices derogatory to the dignity of women and disadvantaged sections of society.

Annexure 7

Code of Conduct for Law Enforcement Officials[1]

(Adopted by United Nations General Assembly Resolution 34/169 of 17th December 1979)

Article 1

Law enforcement officials shall at all times fulfil the duty imposed upon them by law, by serving the community and by protecting all persons against illegal acts, consistent with the high degree of responsibility required by their profession.

Commentary

(a) The term 'law enforcement officials', includes all officers of the law, whether appointed or elected, who exercise police powers, especially the powers of arrest or detention.

(b) In countries where police powers are exercised by military authorities, whether uniformed or not, or by State security forces, the definition of law enforcement officials shall be regarded as including officers of such services.

(c) Service to the community is intended to include particularly the rendition of services of assistance to those members of the community who by reason of personal, economic, social or other emergencies are in need of immediate aid.

---

1. Available at the website: http://www.ohchr.org/EN/ProfessionalInterest/Pages/LawEnforcementOfficials.aspx (last visited on 17/09/2014).

(d) This provision is intended to cover not only all violent, predatory and harmful acts, but extends to the full range of prohibitions under penal statutes. It extends to conduct by persons not capable of incurring criminal liability.

Article 2

In the performance of their duty, law enforcement officials shall respect and protect human dignity and maintain and uphold the human rights of all persons.

Commentary

(a) The human rights in question are identified and protected by national and international law. Among the relevant international instruments are the Universal Declaration of Human Rights, the International Covenant on Civil and Political Rights, the Declaration on the Protection of All Persons from Being Subjected to Torture and Other Cruel, Inhuman or Degrading Treatment or Punishment, the United Nations Declaration on the Elimination of All Forms of Racial Discrimination, the International Convention on the Elimination of All Forms of Racial Discrimination, the International Convention on the Suppression and Punishment of the Crime of Apartheid, the Convention on the Prevention and Punishment of the Crime of Genocide, the Standard Minimum Rules for the Treatment of Prisoners and the Vienna Convention on Consular Relations.

(b) National commentaries to this provision should indicate regional or national provisions identifying and protecting these rights.

Article 3

Law enforcement officials may use force only when strictly necessary and to the extent required for the performance of their duty.

Commentary

(a) This provision emphasizes that the use of force by law enforcement officials should be exceptional; while it implies that law enforcement officials may be authorized to use force as is reasonably necessary under the circumstances for the prevention of crime or in effecting or assisting in the lawful arrest of offenders or suspected offenders, no force going beyond that may be used.

(b) National law ordinarily restricts the use of force by law enforcement officials in accordance with a principle of proportionality. It is to be understood that such national principles of proportionality are to be respected in the interpretation of this provision. In no case should this provision be interpreted to authorize the use of force which is disproportionate to the legitimate objective to be achieved.

(c) The use of firearms is considered an extreme measure. Every effort should be made to exclude the use of firearms, especially against children. In general, firearms should not be used except when a suspected offender offers armed resistance or otherwise jeopardizes the lives of others and less extreme measures are not sufficient to restrain or apprehend the suspected offender. In every instance in which a firearm is discharged, a report should be made promptly to the competent authorities.

Article 5

No law enforcement official may inflict, instigate or tolerate any act of torture or other cruel, inhuman or degrading treatment or punishment, nor may any law enforcement official invoke superior orders or exceptional circumstances such as a state of war or a threat of war, a threat to national security, internal political instability or any other public emergency as a justification of torture or other cruel, inhuman or degrading treatment or punishment.

Commentary

(a) This prohibition derives from the Declaration on the Protection of All Persons from Being Subjected to Torture and Other Cruel, Inhuman or Degrading Treatment or Punishment, adopted by the General Assembly, according to which:

> "[Such an act is] an offence to human dignity and shall be condemned as a denial of the purposes of the Charter of the United Nations and as a violation of the human rights and fundamental freedoms proclaimed in the Universal Declaration of Human Rights [and other international human rights instruments]."

(b) The Declaration defines torture as follows:

> "... torture means any act by which severe pain or suffering, whether physical or mental, is intentionally inflicted by or at the instigation of a public official on a person for such purposes as obtaining from him or a third person information or confession, punishing him for an act he has committed or is suspected of having committed, or intimidating him or other persons. It does not include pain or suffering arising only from, inherent in or incidental to, lawful sanctions to the extent consistent with the Standard Minimum Rules for the Treatment of Prisoners."

(c) The term 'cruel, inhuman or degrading treatment or punishment' has not been defined by the General Assembly but should be interpreted so as to extend the widest possible protection against abuses, whether physical or mental.

Article 6

Law enforcement officials shall ensure the full protection of the health of persons in their custody and, in particular, shall take immediate action to secure medical attention whenever required.

Commentary

(a) 'Medical attention', which refers to services rendered by any medical personnel, including certified medical practitioners and paramedics, shall be secured when needed or requested.

(b) While the medical personnel are likely to be attached to the law enforcement operation, law enforcement officials must take into account the judgment of such personnel when they recommend providing the person in custody with appropriate treatment through, or in consultation with, medical personnel from outside the law enforcement operation.

(c) It is understood that law enforcement officials shall also secure medical attention for victims of violations of law or of accidents occurring in the course of violations of law.

Article 8

Law enforcement officials shall respect the law and the present Code. They shall also, to the best of their capability, prevent and rigorously oppose any violations of them.

Law enforcement officials who have reason to believe that a violation of the present Code has occurred or is about to occur shall report the matter to their superior authorities and, where necessary, to other appropriate authorities or organs vested with reviewing or remedial power.

Commentary

(a) This Code shall be observed whenever it has been incorporated into national legislation or practice. If legislation or practice contains stricter provisions than those of the present Code, those stricter provisions shall be observed.

(b) The article seeks to preserve the balance between the need for internal discipline of the agency on which public safety is largely dependent, on the one hand, and the need for dealing with violations of basic human rights, on the other. Law enforcement officials shall report violations within the chain of command and take other lawful action outside the chain of command only when no other remedies are available or effective. It is understood that law enforcement officials shall not suffer administrative or other penalties because they have reported that a violation of this Code has occurred or is about to occur.

(c) The term 'appropriate authorities or organs vested with reviewing or remedial power' refers to any authority or organ existing under national law, whether internal to the law enforcement agency or independent thereof, with statutory, customary or other power to review grievances and complaints arising out of violations within the purview of this Code.

(d) In some countries, the mass media may be regarded as performing complaint review functions similar to those described in sub-paragraph (c) above. Law enforcement officials may, therefore, be justified if, as a last resort and in accordance with the laws and customs of their own countries and with the provisions of article 4 of the present Code, they bring violations to the attention of public opinion through the mass media.

(e) Law enforcement officials who comply with the provisions of this Code deserve the respect, the full support and the co-operation of the community and of the law enforcement agency in which they serve, as well as the law enforcement profession.

Annexure 8

Basic Principles on the Use of Force and Firearms by Law Enforcement Officials[1]

(Adopted by the Eighth United Nations Congress on the Prevention of Crime and the Treatment of Offenders, Havana, Cuba, 27th August to 7th September 1990)

Whereas the work of law enforcement officials is a social service of great importance and there is, therefore, a need to maintain and, whenever necessary, to improve the working conditions and status of these officials,

Whereas a threat to the life and safety of law enforcement officials must be seen as a threat to the stability of society as a whole,

Whereas law enforcement officials have a vital role in the protection of the right to life, liberty and security of the person, as guaranteed in the Universal Declaration of Human Rights and reaffirmed in the International Covenant on Civil and Political Rights,

Whereas the Standard Minimum Rules for the Treatment of Prisoners provide for the circumstances in which prison officials may use force in the course of their duties,

Whereas article 3 of the Code of Conduct for Law Enforcement Officials provides that law enforcement officials may use force only when strictly necessary and to the extent required for the performance of their duty,

---

1. Available at the website: http://www.ohchr.org/EN/ProfessionalInterest/Pages/UseOfForceAndFirearms.aspx (last visited on 17/09/2014).

Whereas the preparatory meeting for the Seventh United Nations Congress on the Prevention of Crime and the Treatment of Offenders, held at Vienna, Italy, agreed on elements to be considered in the course of further work on restraints on the use of force and firearms by law enforcement officials,

Whereas the Seventh Congress, in its resolution 14, inter alia, emphasizes that the use of force and firearms by law enforcement officials should be commensurate with due respect for human rights,

Whereas the Economic and Social Council, in its resolution 1986/10, section IX, of 21st May 1986, invited Member States to pay particular attention in the implementation of the Code to the use of force and firearms by law enforcement officials, and the General Assembly, in its resolution 41/149 of 4th December 1986, inter alia, welcomed this recommendation made by the Council,

Whereas it is appropriate that, with due regard to their personal safety, consideration be given to the role of law enforcement officials in relation to the administration of justice, to the protection of the right to life, liberty and security of the person, to their responsibility to maintain public safety and social peace and to the importance of their qualifications, training and conduct,

The basic principles set forth below, which have been formulated to assist Member States in their task of ensuring and promoting the proper role of law enforcement officials, should be taken into account and respected by governments within the framework of their national legislation and practice, and be brought to the attention of law enforcement officials as well as other persons, such as judges, prosecutors, lawyers, members of the executive branch and the legislature, and the public.

General Provisions

1. Governments and law enforcement agencies shall adopt and implement rules and regulations on the use of force and firearms against persons by law enforcement officials. In developing such rules and regulations, governments and law enforcement agencies shall keep the ethical issues associated with the use of force and firearms constantly under review.
2. Governments and law enforcement agencies should develop a range of means as broad as possible and equip law enforcement officials with various types of weapons and ammunition that would allow for a differentiated use of force and firearms. These should include the development of non-lethal incapacitating weapons for use in appropriate situations, with a view to increasingly restraining the application of means capable of causing death or injury to persons. For the same purpose, it should also be possible for law enforcement officials to be equipped with self-defensive equipment such as shields, helmets, bullet-proof vests and bullet-proof means of transportation, in order to decrease the need to use weapons of any kind.
3. The development and deployment of non-lethal incapacitating weapons should be carefully evaluated in order to minimize the risk of endangering uninvolved persons, and the use of such weapons should be carefully controlled.
4. Law enforcement officials, in carrying out their duty, shall, as far as possible, apply non-violent means before resorting to the use of force and firearms. They may use force and firearms only if other means remain ineffective or without any promise of achieving the intended result.
5. Whenever the lawful use of force and firearms is unavoidable, law enforcement officials shall:

(a) Exercise restraint in such use and act in proportion to the seriousness of the offence and the legitimate objective to be achieved;

(b) Minimize damage and injury, and respect and preserve human life;

(c) Ensure that assistance and medical aid are rendered to any injured or affected persons at the earliest possible moment;

(d) Ensure that relatives or close friends of the injured or affected person are notified at the earliest possible moment.

6. Where injury or death is caused by the use of force and firearms by law enforcement officials, they shall report the incident promptly to their superiors, in accordance with principle 22.

7. Governments shall ensure that arbitrary or abusive use of force and firearms by law enforcement officials is punished as a criminal offence under their law.

8. Exceptional circumstances such as internal political instability or any other public emergency may not be invoked to justify any departure from these basic principles.

Special Provisions

9. Law enforcement officials shall not use firearms against persons except in self-defence or defence of others against the imminent threat of death or serious injury, to prevent the perpetration of a particularly serious crime involving grave threat to life, to arrest a person presenting such a danger and resisting their authority, or to prevent his or her escape, and only when less extreme means are insufficient to achieve these objectives. In any event,

intentional lethal use of firearms may only be made when strictly unavoidable in order to protect life.

10. In the circumstances provided for under principle 9, law enforcement officials shall identify themselves as such and give a clear warning of their intent to use firearms, with sufficient time for the warning to be observed, unless to do so would unduly place the law enforcement officials at risk or would create a risk of death or serious harm to other persons, or would be clearly inappropriate or pointless in the circumstances of the incident.

11. Rules and regulations on the use of firearms by law enforcement officials should include guidelines that:

    (a) Specify the circumstances under which law enforcement officials are authorized to carry firearms and prescribe the types of firearms and ammunition permitted;

    (b) Ensure that firearms are used only in appropriate circumstances and in a manner likely to decrease the risk of unnecessary harm;

    (c) Prohibit the use of those firearms and ammunition that cause unwarranted injury or present an unwarranted risk;

    (d) Regulate the control, storage and issuing of firearms, including procedures for ensuring that law enforcement officials are accountable for the firearms and ammunition issued to them;

    (e) Provide for warnings to be given, if appropriate, when firearms are to be discharged;

    (f) Provide for a system of reporting whenever law enforcement officials use firearms in the performance of their duty.

Policing Persons in Custody or Detention

15. Law enforcement officials, in their relations with persons in custody or detention, shall not use force, except when strictly necessary for the maintenance of security and order within the institution, or when personal safety is threatened.
16. Law enforcement officials, in their relations with persons in custody or detention, shall not use firearms, except in self-defence or in the defence of others against the immediate threat of death or serious injury, or when strictly necessary to prevent the escape of a person in custody or detention presenting the danger referred to in principle 9.
17. The preceding principles are without prejudice to the rights, duties and responsibilities of prison officials, as set out in the Standard Minimum Rules for the Treatment of Prisoners, particularly rules 33, 34 and 54.

Reporting and Review Procedures

24. Governments and law enforcement agencies shall ensure that superior officers are held responsible if they know, or should have known, that law enforcement officials under their command are resorting, or have resorted, to the unlawful use of force and firearms, and they did not take all measures in their power to prevent, suppress or report such use.

25. Governments and law enforcement agencies shall ensure that no criminal or disciplinary sanction is imposed on law enforcement officials who, in compliance with the Code of Conduct for Law Enforcement Officials and these basic principles, refuse to carry out an order to use force and firearms, or who report such use by other officials.

26. Obedience to superior orders shall be no defence if law enforcement officials knew that an order to use force and firearms resulting in the death or serious injury of a person was manifestly unlawful and had a reasonable opportunity to refuse to follow it. In any case, responsibility also rests on the superiors who gave the unlawful orders.

In accordance with the commentary to article 1 of the Code of Conduct for Law Enforcement Officials, the term 'law enforcement officials' includes all officers of the law, whether appointed or elected, who exercise police powers, especially the powers of arrest or detention. In countries where police powers are exercised by military authorities, whether uniformed or not, or by State security forces, the definition of law enforcement officials shall be regarded as including officers of such services.

Annexure 9

Extract of Judgment of the Andhra Pradesh High Court[1]

Extract of Judgment of the Hon'ble High Court of Andhra Pradesh in the case Andhra Pradesh Civil Liberties Committee *vs* The Government of Andhra Pradesh in the writ petition Nos. 15419 of 2006; 26358 of 1999; 7906 of 2000; 14475 of 2002; 440 of 2003 and 857 of 2008.

Summary of the Factual Matrix of the Cases on Board

WP No 15419 of 2006 is instituted by the Andhra Pradesh Civil Liberties Committee (for short 'the APCLC') for a direction to the concerned police to register a crime into the offence of killing of eight (8) Maoist Naxalites in an alleged encounter that occurred on 23rd July 2006 in the Nallamala forest near Darboina Penta and Nekkanti Palutla villages of Yerragondapalem mandal, Prakasam district, by registering a case under Section 302 of the Indian Penal Code, 1860 (for short 'the IPC') against the police personnel who participated in the alleged encounter; to initiate proceedings for their prosecution; to call for all the records with regard to the crime registered on this encounter; and to pass such other order or orders as may be deemed fit and proper in the circumstances of the case.

The sister of one of the deceased Rajitha @ Shyamal filed WP No 857 of 2008 in respect of the same incident as is covered

1. Available at the website: https://docs.google.com/document/d/1PDZlgpCSYLcKipid9yHDNWKnsjO85Ml9O43XcfgLSD8/edit?pli=1 (last visited on 17/08/2013).

by the above writ petition. The petitioner seeks disclosure of the identity of 15 members of District Special Police, SI and PC Nos 430 and 1843 of Yerragondapalem PS and a direction to register a case against the concerned police officers u/s 302 IPC in view of their involvement in the death by encounter of petitioner's sister and 7 others.

WP No 26358 of 1999 is filed for a declaration that the inaction of the respondents Nos 3 and 6 in proceeding under law against the concerned Police officers of the 1st respondent PS (for having opened fire without provocation thereby severely injuring the petitioner's husband on 15th June 1999 evening at Gajasingavaram, Gambhirraopet Mandal, Karimnagar district) and failing to take financial and other responsibility for the medical care and well being of the injured, is arbitrary and illegal; for a direction to the 6th respondent to provide adequate medical treatment; for compensation in an amount of ₹ 2 lakh towards damages and costs of the medical expenses incurred; and for a further direction to the respondents 3 and 6 to prosecute the concerned police personnel of the 1st respondent PS in accordance with law.

WP No 7906 of 2000 also is by the APCLC for preservation of the bodies of the persons killed in an encounter that occurred in Kaukonda Hills, Parkal Mandal, Warangal district; for handing over the bodies to the family members after identification; and for a direction to register a crime u/s 302 IPC.

WP No 14475 of 2002 is again by the APCLC to direct the 6th respondent to register a case u/s 302 r/w Sec 34 IPC against the respondents 1 to 5; direction to the State (R-7) to entrust the investigation in the said case to the CBI (R-18) in relation to the death in encounter of one Durga Prasad @ Pilli Prasad at Vijayawada on 7th June 2002; and for suitable compensation to the family members of the deceased. The deceased Durga Prasad was arrested by the Vuyyur Town Police on 19th May

2002 in connection with Cr No 75/02 alleging his involvement in the murder of Sirikonda Venkanna. According to the version of the State during the course of investigation in Cr No 75/02 Durga Prasad was perceived to be concerned with Cr No 161/02 for the death of one Peyyala Ramu. He was taken into custody in respect of that crime too. While in police custody and in the early hours of 5th June 2002 when the accused Durga Prasad was being escorted out of the police lock up for answering calls of nature he escaped and Cr No 444/02 was registered against him. On 7th June 2002 during the efforts to trace the absconder Durga Prasad and on information the police party proceeded towards Gunadala Railway Station. On the night of 8th June 2002 the police found two persons consuming liquor. On questioning the identity of the two persons, one escaped under the cover of darkness and the other attacked the Inspector with a knife and inflicted bleeding injuries. The SI fired in private defence resulting in instantaneous death. The deceased was identified as Durga Prasad. Thereupon Cr No 448/02 was registered under Sections 332, 307 and 100 r/w 34 IPC and Sec 134 CrPC and investigation taken up.

WP No 440 of 2003 is by the APCLC for preservation of 6 bodies killed in two different alleged 'fake encounters' occurred on 5th January 2003 and 6th January 2003 within the jurisdiction of the respondents 1 and 2 PS; to direct post-mortem by a team of forensic doctors duly videographed; to hand over the bodies to the family members; and to register a case u/s 302 IPC against the Police Officers involved in the two incidents.

WP No 15419 of 2006 (the lead writ petition) was admitted on 27th September 2006 and certain interlocutory directives were issued. By way of WPMP No 20579 of 2007 the petitioner sought a direction to the respondent Nos 3, 5 and 8 to reveal the names of the members of the police special party who participated in the operations that resulted in the death of eight (8) Maoist Naxalites on 23rd July 2006. This court by an order dated 30th July 2007 rejected this application on the ground that the petitioner had made no such request to the concerned authority under the Right to Information Act, 2005 (for short 'the Information Act, 2005').

The petitioner submitted an application on 1st August 2007 to the 3rd and 5th respondents and the Deputy Superintendent of Police, Gurajala, Guntur district, the Investigating Officer in Cr No 30 of 2006 for particulars of the police officers who participated in the encounter. The 5th respondent who is the designated Information Officer under the Information Act 2005 rejected the application on 30th August 2007. The petitioner thereupon filed WPMP No 29843 of 2007 for a direction to the respondents to reveal the names of the police officers. In response thereto, the first respondent-State filed WPMP No 31250 of 2007 claiming privilege under Section 123 of the Indian Evidence Act regarding disclosure of names, on the ground that it would adversely affect the security, law and order in the State.

On 31st December 2007 while considering the draft issues presented on behalf of the petitioner, this court granted liberty to all the parties to file their respective draft issues. After hearing the learned counsel for the respective parties and considering the draft issues, this Bench on 7th February 2008 framed the following issues for consideration:

Issues

1. Where a police officer causes the death of a person, acting or purporting to act in discharge of official duties or in self-defence as the case may be, is there commission of a cognizable offence (including in an appropriate case the offence of culpable homicide); and whether the information relating to such circumstances requires to be registered as a First

Information Report obligating investigation in accordance with the procedure prescribed by the Code of Criminal Procedure, 1973?

2. Whether the existence of circumstances bringing a case within any of the exceptions in the Indian Penal Code, 1860 including exercise of the Right of Private Defence be could conclusively determined during investigation; whether the final report submitted by the police officer to the Magistrate on completion of the investigation is conclusive or whether the existence of the circumstances coming within the exceptions requires to be determined only in appropriate judicial proceedings?
3. Whether a magisterial enquiry (whether under the Code of Criminal Procedure or extant Police Standing Orders) into the cause and circumstances of death occasioned by an act of a police officer obviate the rigor of investigation and trial of such act?
4. Whether the State, the police establishment or a police officer is immune from an obligation to disclose the identity of a Police Officer who had committed an act causing the death of a person, to enable an investigating officer or any person aggrieved by such death to effectively seek justice; and if so, in what circumstances or contexts?

Summation

To conclude, we hold:

(A) **On issue No 1:** That where a police officer causes death of a person, acting or purporting to act in discharge of official duties or in self-defence as the case may be, the first information relating to such circumstance (even when by a Police/Public Official; whether an alleged perpetrator is named or not) shall be recorded and registered as FIR, enumerating the relevant provisions of Law, (u/s 154(1) CrPC) and shall be investigated (u/s 156/157 CrPC).

(B) **On issue No 2:** That the existence of circumstances bringing a case within any of the Exceptions in the Indian Penal Code including the exercise of the Right of Private Defence (a General Exception in Chapter IV IPC), cannot be conclusively determined during investigation. The opinion recorded by the Investigating Officer in the final report forwarded to the Magistrate (u/s 173 CrPC), is only an opinion. Such opinion shall be considered by the Magistrate in the context of the record of investigation together with the material and evidence collected during the course of investigation. The Magistrate (notwithstanding an opinion of the Investigating officer, that no cognizable offence appears to have been committed; that one or more or all of the accused are not culpable; or that the investigation discloses that the death of civilian(s) in a police encounter is not culpable in view of legitimate exercise by the police of the Right of Private Defence), shall critically examine the entirety of the evidence collected during investigation to ascertain whether the opinion of the Investigating Officer is borne out by the record of investigation. The Magistrate has the discretion to disregard the opinion and take cognizance of the offence u/s 190 CrPC.

(C) **On issue No 3:** That a magisterial enquiry (inquest) (u/Ss 174 to 176 CrPC) is neither a substitute nor an alternative to the obligation to record the information as FIR and to conduct investigation into the facts and circumstances of the case and if necessary to take measures for the discovery and arrest of the offender(s) (u/Ss 154(1), 156 and 157 CrPC), and

(D) **On issue No 4:** In view of the conclusions on issues Nos 1 to 3 and in view of our declaration [that the information conveyed to the officer in charge of a Police Station (u/s 154(1) CrPC) or a complaint made to the Magistrate (u/Chpt XV, Sec 200 CrPC), need not mention the name of the Police Officer(s) who the complainant believes is the perpetrator of the offence complained of], it is not necessary to pronounce on whether the State, the Police Establishment or a Police Officer has immunity from the obligation to disclose the identity (of a police officer who had committed an act causing the death of a person), to a person aggrieved by such death to effectively seek justice. Whether the investigating officer is required to disclose the names of the police officers who are involved in an operation resulting in civilian casualty when a request for such information is lodged by an individual, is an issue not within the spectrum of the issues falling for our determination herein. This aspect is left open. The obligation to disclose to the Investigating Officer the identity of the police officer(s) so involved, is however absolute and there is no immunity whatsoever from this obligation. Withholding of any information or material that impedes effective or expeditious investigation violates several provisions of the Indian Penal Code and the Criminal Procedure Code (pointed out in our analyses on this issue).

Dated: 6th February 2009

Index